GIRL AND HER THERAPIST

Release the Shame

Eugenia A. Franklin-Springer

ESProductions

Copyright © 2012 Eugenia A. Franklin-Springer

All rights reserved

ISBN-13: 9781481091374

Cover design by: Cover Creator
Printed in the United States of America

Contact: journeybooks43@gmail.com

Dedicated

To

You who have suffered too long In fearful silence, shame, and pain. Now is the time to reclaim your dignity. Now is the time to let go the pain and shame. No more secrets! Start talking. Talk yourself out of the pain, out of the shame.

<>

"Get this—no matter what is playing out in your life right now, you can at this moment take control of your will, and turn your life in the direction you want to go."

. . . THE AUTHOR

INTRODUCTION

This has been a difficult book for me to write. Truly living is traveling along a path of unfolding awareness.

In these pages, I am reaching out to survivors of sexual abuse still hurting and trying to cope. I want you to know that you don't have to be suffering. You can transcend the guilt, shame, resentment, hate, loathing, and pain. In Part Three of this book I show you how.

In the year 2000 as I prepared to publish a small collection of my writings, "Words of Wisdom from a Caribbean Woman", I knew I had to address the problem of sexual abuse in general and incest in particular.

A few years earlier I had returned to the country of my birth after a twenty year absence. Steeped in my search for meaning and purpose in life, I, with a terminal degree in biology, was discovering, as I immersed myself in the area of interpersonal relationships, that many among us had been victims of sexual violation.

Memories of having been involved in sexual activity forced on them, were haunting them., even as shame prevented them from talking out, and exposing the perpetrator.

If only to contribute to the removal of the shroud of secrecy and self-loathing under which many who shared their story with me, suffered, I had to write this book.

Initially, what unfolded as I put pen to paper, back there in the year, 2000, was the dialogue, "**Girl and Her Therapist**".

Drumming through my very being was the conviction that

our suffering victims had to tell their stories.

Through this dialogue I had to get their story out from under that heavy porous shroud of secrecy.

Incorporated in this dialogue through which I wanted to shake up the awareness of everybody, were the contents of a very vivid dream I had around the time I was feeling impelled to be a voice for all these lovely persons who had confided in me their secret shame. In that dream I saw the poolside described by the **Girl** as she recovered from her long bout of *selective amnesia*.

Here in 2012, I have gone a step further by addressing the problem of sexual abuse—specifically incest—under a wider umbrella--this publication, *Girl and Her Therapist*.

In this work, *Girl and Her Therapist*, I've pulled together elements from various narratives shared with me over the years. I've pulled them all into this one *sexual abuse narrative, Girl and Her Therapist*.

My purpose in writing this book is to do two things: One, sensitize the reader to some of the issues a survivor of sexual abuse might be forced to work through, as he/she struggles to survive under that heavy shroud of secrecy and shame; and two, say to those still traumatized from any type of abuse, that they must come out from hiding, and find relief.

No one has to settle for a troubled life. No one must allow any person or any situation to forever deprive them of the joy of living.

Part One and Part Two of this publication specifically address the therapeutic work of a survivor of sexual abuse.

I warn you, just as having their dignity transgressed is not a pleasant experience for any to recall, so my attempt to expose the gut wrenching disgust, and pain of the victim, is not pleasant to read. But nothing depicted in the **Girl's** awakened memory is an exaggeration. The truth needs to be told.

Abuse disrupts the harmony of mind, and therefore the harmony of every aspect of the victim's life. Healing, therefore, must disrupt that disruption, and restore harmony to that life.

We must fling off that porous shroud of secrecy covering the painful shame of victims and the secret shame of perpetrators and abusers.

Through this publication, **Girl and Her Therapist**, I am lifting off that porous shroud.

Flinging it off is up to all of us..

To abusers, and perpetrators, I say, that for you also, there is hope. Personal boundaries are to be respected. Your sexual needs are your responsibility. Keep your horniness to yourself. Discipline yourself, but spare others--humans, and animals--the indignity of your sexual assaults.

We can, together, build a society in which each of us feels comfortable and safe. We build such a society as you and I commit ourselves to at all times **do the right thing**. From here on, I commit myself to **at all times, do the right thing**. If I lapse, I will pick up myself and return to **right conduct.** But no lapse of mine must ever transgress the **personal boundaries** of another.

es

PART ONE

Woman and Her Therapist

WOMAN AND HER THERAPIST

Woman:

Do I look like a pushover?

Therapist:

You are wondering if you are a pushover.

Woman:

I never thought of myself as a pushover. Everyone knows I am a pliable person. At least that is how I think of myself—pliable and generous. That pretty much sums up who I am. My opinions are not rigid. Anyone can easily persuade me to see things from their perspective. And I consider myself generous. If somebody wants something I have they won't have to beg or pressure me. If I could give it, I give it.

Therapist:

Okay . . .

Woman:

Like with people in my office, as long as I could, I help out.

Therapist:

If the people in your office want anything from you as long as you could give it, you give it?

Woman:

Something like that. My coworkers say I am the sweetest person. Whatever they want from me they get. I wish they were as considerate of me.

Therapist:

You give whatever your coworkers ask for, but they won't facilitate you if you need their help?

Woman:

None of them cares for me, really, although they are always

asking for one favor or another. Either they want me to cover for them, or they want to borrow money, or they want me to buy lunch for them. They are always asking for some favor. It's like they feel obligated to ask for one favor or another.

Therapist:

You lend your money to people even though you feel they don't care for you . . .?

Woman:

Maybe if I give them what they want they would like me. I feel so ashamed when people say bad things about me. Though I know what they say is not true, I feel guilty; so I do whatever I can to discourage people from talking about me. My fiancé says I am a pushover. Maybe I am . . . He wants to move in. . . .

Therapist:

Your fiancé wants to move into your home?

Woman:

Yes. I have my own home. He is not really my fiancé. We are not engaged. He uses my vehicle. Now, when I want to use my vehicle I have to call him so many times before he brings it, and then he comes for it as soon as I am back.

Therapist:

You seem agitated . . . distressed . . .

Woman:

I want this man to stop coming to my house. I want him to stop using my vehicle, and to get out of my life.

Therapist:

I hear you saying you want the man out of your house and out of your life . . .

Woman:

I'm so afraid . . . afraid and ashamed.

Therapist:

Afraid, and ashamed?

Woman:

I'm afraid the man would make a brawl and become violent. He seems to be the type. I am ashamed because I keep making a fool of myself. People who know me ask how an educated woman like I could choose to be with a man who has nothing going for him . . . I don't need anything from this man. I thought if I let him share what I own he would respect me, and perhaps even love me.

Therapist:

You thought that by being kind to this man you could get him to love you?

Woman:

I have a lovely home—a beautiful home. This man behaves as though he provided my home and everything else that I own, even my vehicle. This man has never given me even one penny, yet he uses my vehicle as though he owns it. He even demands money to put fuel in the car. And I am such a pushover; I give him whatever he demands. He looks so hostile, I'm afraid to tell him no, or to tell him just go and leave me alone. Help me, please. Help me understand why I form intimate relationships with people who are only out to use me.

Therapist:

You feel that everyone with whom you have had an intimate relationship was just out to use you?

Woman:

I am nice to everybody. Why won't people like me just for my sake, and not only for what they can get from me? What's wrong with me? Even my mother seems to dislike me.

Therapist:

You believe your mother dislikes you?

Woman:

My mother used to visit. She stopped when this man started

coming regularly to my home. I don't blame her. This man would disrespect anybody... I won't want him disrespecting my mother.

Therapist:

You are saying that it is important to you that this man does not disrespect your mother ...?

Woman:

What? What man? I ... I don't talk about him. I don't want to talk about him!

Therapist:

Okay ... Something I said triggered off this agitated response? I hear you saying you don't want to talk about this man; so we won't talk about him.

Woman:

I feel afraid and weak when I think about him. I am not sure why. I don't know why, but I don't like him at all. My blood crawls whenever I see him. The sight of him makes me sick.

Therapist:

You don't like this man at all ...

Woman:

I feel suffocated—claustrophobic—whenever I think of being even in the same house with him. God, forgive me, but I think I hate that man. The way I feel, I think if he dies, I won't be sorry.

Therapist:

You won't be unduly upset if your fiancé dies—you hate him so much?

Woman:

My fiancé? Why would you ask that? I said I want him out of my life. That doesn't mean I want him dead.

Therapist:

Okay.

Woman:

My mother is always angry. She quarrels and throws words at my father.

Therapist:

Your mother is angry at your father?

Woman:

Not only at my father . . . She throws words at me also. My mother is an angry woman, a very angry woman. I love her, but she seems to be having a hard time showing any kind of affection to me. She never even hugs me.

Therapist:

You wish your mother would hug you?

Woman:

We used to be close. I am her only child. I remember when she used to laugh with me, but I have no memory of her smiling with me in my teen years. I became very afraid of her . . . Try as I may I can't figure out why. She is all I have.

Therapist:

Your mother is all you have . . .? No father? No sibling? No pet?

Woman:

Don't! Please don't . . .!

Therapist:

Go ahead . . . Weep. You are safe here. Right now you are very safe. You are sobbing so hard . . . Tell me what you don't want me to do, or ask. You are weeping so hysterically; I am wondering if something I said triggered off all this.

Woman:

What's wrong with me? I feel like I'm going mad! I feel like you punched me in my solar plexus just now—like you gripped my gut and yanked it . . .

Therapist:

Can you say exactly what triggered off this very agitated response?

Woman:

I don't know. O God, I don't know. Please help me. Memory goes back only so far, then nothing—Nothing! Yet I keep reacting. This happens often—I hear or see something, and I have these crazy reactions that I suppress till I could be alone. Memory extends only so far, then absolutely nothing!

Therapist:

Nothing?

Woman:

Nothing.

Therapist:

Memory goes back only so far?

Woman:

I remember clearly when I was taking classes in Business Management. I'd go to classes, and when I got back home either my mother would be there, or she would have left food for me. She was so angry, though . . . always so angry.

Therapist:

Sometimes your mother was not at home when you returned from classes. Whenever she was not at home she would have left food for you?

Woman:

I was living on my own, at my apartment.

Therapist:

Your memory takes you back to living on your own at your apartment . . .?

Woman:

My memory about the day I moved into my apartment is clear. My mother helped me fix it up.

Therapist:

And that is as far back as your memory takes you—to your mother helping you fix up your apartment after she had helped you move into it?

Woman:

I remember lovely childhood days with my parents . . . graduating from elementary school and starting high school . . . then memory gets fuzzy before the blank. And I have this recurring dream. Not really a dream . . . more like a nightmare . . .

Therapist:

Memory gets fuzzy before the blank, and you've been having a recurring nightmare?

Woman:

Yes, memory gets fuzzy—like whatever I'm trying to recall is right here in my mind, but keeps eluding recall—keeps slipping back into forgetfulness.

Therapist:

And then you would have this nightmare?

Woman:

I would see this friendly puppy, this little dog, trotting towards me, and as it gets close enough to recognize me, it would transform itself into a hideous creature, right there before my eyes.

Therapist:

Hideous creature?

Woman:

. . . A horrible, diabolic, heavy-set, wild canine creature. While I am watching it, this creature would bare its teeth at me, and shriek so piercingly I would be paralyzed with horror. Then I would watch it, shrieking still, slowly turn around, and powerfully slink away. It slinks away with a slow, diabolic stride—shrieking with every step. Sometimes the scenario would change, but no matter how the scenario changes, the puppy, whether it is in the arms of somebody I meet, or shown on my television screen, would react the same way. If it is in somebody's arms, it would jump to the ground as soon as it looks closely enough at me to recognize me, then it would morph into this little monstrous form, bare its teeth, let out this diabolic shriek, and then slowly slink away, diabolically shrieking with every step.

Therapist:

Even when it is seeing you from your television screen the Puppy would slink away shrieking as though in distress?

Woman:

Even if it is in someone's arms, it would jump down from the person's arms, morph into this horrible looking creature, bare its teeth, then slink away from me, shrieking still.

Therapist:

You have broken out into a cold sweat. Right now, you are safe.

Woman:

There is no sound as horrible as that shrieking, not in real life. The shrieking is not a sound of distress . . .

Therapist:

It's not?

Woman:

No, it does not sound like an animal in distress.
The creature looks like a distorted, demonic thing—like a menacing creature from hell. It moves with the slow, powerful stride of a demonic canine creature. Right there before my eyes, between the time I first glance at the puppy, and the time it takes for the puppy to recognize me and turn away from me—within that short space of time—it kind of morphs into a furious demonic, canine creature. And the frightening sound it makes is a powerful, teeth grinding,

demonic kind of shriek. I would jump up from my sleep, in cold sweat, terrified that this fiendish creature—this evil thing—would jump on me and shred me to bits.

Therapist:

And the pet . . . There is that agitation again. . . .. Is the animal that turns away from you and morphs into this evil-looking creature, ever a feline creature, or is it always a canine?

Woman:

It is always a dog, always a puppy. Please can you help me recover that blanked out part of my memory? I am afraid of hypnosis. Is there some other way you could help me recover that blank in my memory?

Therapist:

You want me to help you recover that blank in your memory, but you do not want me using hypnosis?

Woman:

That's correct. Can you use any method other than hypnosis?

Therapist:

We can use reverie.

Woman:

Reverie?

Therapist:

I will count down from ten to one. By the time I reach one, your eyes will be closed. I will ask you to recall certain memories, and then we will get to your blocked engrams. You will be, as it were, in a deep sleep, but you will be in charge throughout this process. If you want to snap out of reverie, you would be able to. However, I will do this on one condition . . .

Woman:

What condition?

Therapist:

You must agree to continue with the stipulated number of sessions. And we must meet every day till the sessions are completed.

Woman:

Why can't I stop having sessions if I want to?

Therapist:

Your body has a reason for burying part of your past deep in your subconscious. What you might be suffering from is a class of functional amnesia known as selective amnesia. We have to be gentle with your mind, and help you cope with whatever you have hidden away in your subconscious. If I am not allowed to work with you till the engram loses its sting, I would have put you at risk. I need to know that you understand clearly what I just said.

Woman:

I hear you saying that if we start reverie, we must complete the requisite number of sessions; if we don't, I could go mad, or become really sick.

Therapist:

If we do not complete the number of sessions, I might not be able to clear the engrams we unearth. You could then be on your own to cope with the full blown emotional, mental, and physical response to whatever it is your mind has hidden away from your conscious recall all these years.

Woman:

I would sign whatever you want me to sign. But first, please tell me, how can reverie help me cope with whatever I seem to be repressing?

Therapist:

Once you retrieve that block of memory you have repressed, I will take you through the story, into all its little handles that so readily get hooked. You will recognize what in your repressed memory has been triggering off all those responses that puzzle you. We will find that block of repressed memory and drain it of all distressing emotions. In time, you'll be able to recall whatever incident or incidents you have repressed ...

Woman:

Right now, I want nothing more.

Therapist:

Let me warn you—you may not like what you recall; however, though you may not like what you recall, you won't be making such a mad dash away from it that you'd be rushing off to bury it. As you stay with the process, you will accept that whatever happened is part of your past—an important part of your past. In time you would come to accept whatever your mind throws up at you—whatever you have been running from.

Woman:

I think I'm ready for reverie.

End of Part 1, Woman and Her Therapist

PART TWO

Girl and Her Therapist

GIRL AND HER THERAPIST

Girl:

I remember this pool. It is next to our house. Look, the crown of the apricot tree. I could see it up there next to the high western wall. I am walking along the apron of the pool, going from north to south. I see two outdoor tables down there, towards the southern end of the apron. The table farthest from me has a poolside lounge chair next to it. 'Looks like somebody was sitting there looking at the pool, and then just got up and left the chair there. Here, near to where I am standing is a pile of bricks—red clay bricks. I walk around the pile of bricks. They are neatly stacked.

Therapist:

You are walking around the pile of bricks?

Girl:

My eyes are fixated on this pile of bricks.

Therapist:

You have an interest in these bricks?

Girl:

They can be used to build; they can also destroy. Something has been building up inside me . . .

Therapist:

Something?

Girl:

A powerful desire to destroy. My body is aching for the excitement of an adrenaline rush.

Therapist:

How old are you?

Girl:

I am seventeen years old. My eyes are fixed on this large column of bricks. I can easily pick up a brick from the side here, but I can't reach those stacked in the middle. . .. An evil idea is forming in my head . . . I am feeling driven—like an addict. I am aching for another adrenaline rush, another kill! I'm on a high. I have to drain blood. Something in me is goading me to destroy—to smash and destroy.

Therapist:

You feel that something in you is pushing you to destroy . . .?

Girl:

I am looking back at a neat little concrete house with a low galvanize roof. I just passed through the gate between that little house, and the high brick wall.

Therapist:

Little house?

Girl:

. . . The pool house. Everything within these walls is immaculately, sparklingly, clean. The clear, blue water; the long, curved pool; the tiled, high walls . . . But there is no apron on the eastern side of the pool—the deepest side. No way out over there. The same light cream colored tile covers the wall and the apron of the pool. . ..

Therapist:

You have been silent for a full minute . . .

Girl:

This is a lie. This immaculately, sparklingly clean poolside is a lie—a big, fat lie! Life is not immaculately clean. No matter how much we wash in the pool! Life is messy. My mind is messy . . .So much here looks familiar . . . I thought this was my home. Now, I am not sure. . ..

Therapist:

You are not sure that this is your home ...?

Girl:

I am not alone ... Stop! Stop! Wait ... This is not my poolside. I thought that was my home out there, outside these walls. I thought that was the apricot tree next to my house, but now I'm not so sure. Something is next to me. Stop! Stop!

Therapist:

You want to stop?

Girl:

Yes! Yes! Stop! Something is standing next to me ... Stop! Stop!

Therapist:

You want to stop?

Girl:

Yes! Yes!

Therapist:

Open your eyes ... You are shaking.

Girl:

Something happened at that poolside. I feel so scared. Why am I shaking? What's wrong with me? What am I afraid of? Why am I so afraid? I don't want to feel afraid.

Therapist:

You don't want to deal with fear right now, so let's deal with some pleasant stuff.

Girl:

I need to know where all this fear is coming from. Why am I trembling in fear?

Therapist:

We will get to that. Let's move you to more pleasant places in your recall... I will be counting down from ten to one. When I reach one, your eyes will be closed. You will be going back into memory. If at any time you feel uncomfortable, let me know and I will pull you out of reverie. . .. Recall the most beautiful experience you've ever had. Think about all perceptions—information picked up by your eyes, your nostrils, your ears, your taste, your sense of touch. Describe the sights, the scents, the sounds, the taste, the feelings—all perceptions.

Girl:

This is beautiful! Mama and Papa are walking me towards a swing. All around the grass is green and soft to walk on. Some boys and girls are chasing one another out there on the playground. Some bigger girls and boys are standing in a group chatting.

Therapist:

How old are you?

Girl:

I am eight years old. Everybody is dressed up. Some girls are wearing jumpers—I'm seeing one yellow jumper, two pink, one white, and two red jumpers. The older girls are wearing jeans and pretty blouses. All the boys are wearing jeans or khaki slacks, and jerseys. We are in an open park. I'm seeing adults a little off in the distance. Other people are in the park. I run to the merry-go-round, and after some time, I head for the swing.

Therapist:

And your parents—where are they?

Girl:

. . . With me at the swing. Mama and Papa are taking turns pushing me. We are laughing. We are chanting the ditty*, *"Daddy, won't you swing me high, swing me high up in the sky! Mommy, won't you join Daddy, let us play as a family . . . I love to run and play outside, go up the ladder and down the slide, run, run, run to the merry-go-round, spinning in the breeze is so much fun!"* Mama and Papa step away from behind the swing and leave me alone to the breeze. But they are keeping their eyes on me. This bigger boy, who was swinging nearby, jumps off his swing, comes behind me, pulls my swing back and gives me a hard push. He is sending my swing way up in the sky. I hold on tight and scream. But Daddy is here easing my swing down gently.

Therapist:

Your Daddy is protecting you from this boy?

Girl:

Daddy tells the boy I am not comfortable going that high. The boy says he is sorry, and goes off. I see two white tents close by. Lots of children and their parents are milling around in both tents. Yellow and green streamers decorate one tent and red and white streamers drape from the ceiling to the sides of the other tent.

Therapist:

Sounds like a festive time.

Girl:

The first tent has about six long tables covered with white table cloths, and decorated with little bunches of tiny yellow and white roses. Chairs are neatly arranged around all the tables. I'm seeing trays and trays of cookies, and colorful small sandwiches, and lots of small plastic cups filled with drinks. The cookies are covered with colored sprinkles—red, white, yellow, blue, pink.

Therapist:

Any odors? Any fragrances?

Girl:

I smell roses. I pull away from Mama and Papa and run to sniff the tiny yellow and white roses lying on the table cloth. I like how Papa smells. He uses cologne with a lemony fragrance. The air is filled with an oniony odor, though. Wild onions grow among the grass. Whenever the grounds-men cut the grass in the park that onion odor fills the air. I also smell cake.

Therapist:

Hmm-mm . . . smelling cake?

Girl:

A yummy smelling yellow cake with soft icing.

Therapist:

You are seeing this cake?

Girl:

No, but Mama loves to buy this cake from the bakery. The next tent has two long tables. I see the boy who pushed me high in the swing. He is Papa's nephew. He is with two other boys. They are admiring a large white cake—the same one with a delicious scent.

Therapist:

What are you wearing?

Girl:

I am wearing a pretty white flouncy dress with small red polka dots.

Therapist:

And your hair—how is it styled?

Girl:

My hair is combed up and tied with a satin red ribbon with long streamers reaching my shoulders. . . .. I am walking towards the boy. He's wearing soft khaki jeans and a white jersey. I reach close to the cake, and jump, because the three boys swing around and shout, Happy Birthday! All the people in the tents join in singing, *Happy Birthday to You*. Then everybody look at me and with one voice shout, "Happy Birthday, Sherry!" Mama is smiling with me, and Papa is lifting me high and laughing with me. I hear chuckles all around, and I see smiling faces. I like how Papa smells. He always wears this cologne. Papa is so gentle with me. . . .. This is the largest cake I have ever seen—about three feet by four feet. Little red rose buds made from icing, decorate the edges of this huge cake.

Therapist:

The cake is covered with white icing?

Girl:

Frosty white, soft icing. I whisper to Papa that I feel like putting my open palm on the cake.

Therapist:

On the soft icing . . .?

Girl:

Papa laughs and tells me to go ahead. Everybody laughs when I leave my hand print on the large cake.

Therapist:

Everybody?

Girl:

The people in the tents—Uncle Jack and Uncle Andy. They are Mommy's two brothers. And Papa's older brother, Uncle Wilton, and his wife, Auntie Irma, are also here. My eleven-year-old cousin, Josh—it was he who pushed my swing high —is Uncle Wilton's son. Not one strange face. Everyone is a relative or family friend. I'm hearing lots of laughter, lots of chatter.

Therapist:

On a scale from zero to ten, how happy are you feeling right now?

Girl:

Ten.

Therapist:

Now, recall the most upsetting experience you've had. If at any time you do not want to continue, say, stop, and open your eyes.

Girl:

I am on the apron of the pool, and I am very angry. I'm not alone. Puppy is here with me. I am very angry at Puppy.

Therapist:

You are very angry with your dog?

Girl:

Yes. My dog is a young lovable collie. I call him Puppy. He is here with me. He is on the apron of the pool . . . The apron curves around down at the end. Lovely light goldenrod colored tiles. Puppy is standing quietly next to me. I turn and kick Puppy. I'm kicking him, kicking him, kicking him! He is making me mad!

Therapist:

Puppy is making you mad?

Girl:

He's not fighting back . . .Just struggling to get back on his feet. He's a pushover. He looks so disgusting just slinking away with his tail lowered. I pull my foot back and fire one hard kick! No one should slink away like that.

Therapist:

You want Puppy to fight back?

Girl:

Puppy turns around and looks at me. He growls and snarls. I pull back one foot and swing a hard kick at his head. He yelps and whimpers. All around this pool is enclosed with a high wall, and we are next to a high stack of bricks that go right back to the wall. Puppy is slinking behind the bricks, trying to get away—like a coward. I drag him out. He's just whimpering. I need to kill, to totally destroy something . . . I'm hungry for an adrenalin rush. I'm getting the rush from hearing Puppy's yowl and whine. I have to finish him off. I reach for a brick and I am smashing his head—smashing it, smashing it!

Therapist:

That is a lot of anger—rage. What are you feeling as you smash in Puppy's head?

Girl:

I'm feeling powerful, very powerful. I'm in charge here. I am invincible. Nobody dare try to stop me; nobody dares try to harm me. I will destroy anything that tries to stop me. I am relishing my power. Nobody should just whimper and cowardly slink away. Nobody! Nobody should ever play weak and helpless.

Therapist:

Is Puppy making any attempt to fight back?

Girl:

Yes. When I fired the first kick, Puppy swung around, growled, and snarled. When I fired the next kick—a powerful kick—at his head that was when he dragged himself back up, then slinked away, dragging his tail on the ground.

Therapist:

Your puppy snarled and growled in self-defense?

Girl:

Maybe. I don't know.

Therapist:

Did Puppy ever snarl at you before this?

Girl:

No, never.

Therapist:

Had you ever attacked your Puppy before?

Girl:

No. Puppy is making me mad when he slinks away in a corner and just whimpers. I am so mad I drag him out from behind the pile of bricks. And I am bashing in his head with a brick.

Therapist:

You are bashing in Puppy's head with a brick?

Girl:

Yes. I am bashing it, and bashing it, and bashing it! I am getting my adrenalin rush.

Therapist:

You are looking at your puppy and bashing in its head? What are you seeing as you bash in your puppy's head?

Girl:

This isn't my puppy. This weak, loathsome thing isn't my puppy. This is an evil, ugly thing—pathetically weak. This is a disgraceful and ugly thing. When I scream and beg him to stop, he covers my mouth with his hand and continues hurting me—that filthy, disgusting, evil man with no ears, and no heart! No matter how I scream and beg and plead, he does not hear. I weep but he does not feel my pain. I withdraw into a shell, but he does not see. I loathe the thought of him; I hate that bitch! I hate that sick beast of a man! I hate him! I hate that loathsome, nasty man—that sex maniac beast! Why wasn't my mother at home. . .? I longed for her to stay at home.

Therapist:

If your mother were at home, you would not have felt helpless with your father?

Girl:

He couldn't do me those things if my mother were there. I should have bitten him till he stopped. I should have bitten him and drawn his blood. I should have run out screaming.

Therapist:

You should have fought him off?

Girl:

Nobody should slink away and just whimper like a pathetic victim. I should have scarred him!

Therapist:

You feel you didn't put up enough resistance?

Girl:

How could that happen? How could Puppy understand I was attacking him? I feed Puppy. I play with Puppy. I bathe him. I have always protected Puppy.

Therapist:

Puppy was accustomed to you doing good things to him?

Girl:

Puppy expected me to take care of him. He expected me to be good to him. But what I did wasn't good! O God! What have I done?

Therapist:

It's okay to scream. Go ahead, let it out.

Girl:

I should not have allowed it! O God, I feel wicked! I'm stained! I'm wicked! I'm dirty! I should have killed him. I should have stopped him from using my body for his nastiness!

Therapist:

You feel you are wicked, stained, and dirty because your father had sex with you—because he disrespected and dishonored you?

Girl:

That's what she said . . . Mama said I was dirty. She said I am wicked. I should have fought him off. I should have screamed. But I did scream! I screamed and begged him to stop, but it didn't make any difference. I should have run out the house vomiting out all the nastiness he was pumping inside my head; all the pollution he was spewing on my youth. I should have run outside and screamed it all up. I should have run outside screaming for all the neighbors to hear. Let them know how he was making havoc of my mind—of my life, how he was kicking me up inside my mind. Why didn't I run out the first time and let the whole street know what he had done to me?

Therapist:

You should have exposed your father? You are saying you should have exposed him the first time he violated you—you should not have kept it a secret?

Girl:

He walked like a saint out there. Nobody would have believed me. They would have said I was lying on my father. They would have said my father is a good man, and I am just an ungrateful, wicked child—no one would have believed me.

Therapist:

No one would have believed you?

Girl:

When I threatened to tell Mama, he slapped me and said she would never believe me; that he would say I forced myself on him. . . . Why did I allow myself to become so confused and ashamed? Why? Why? He had me where he wanted me and I gave him my power. Fear kept me under his control. I should have exposed him—that stinking bitch!

Therapist:

Fear of your father gave him the cover to continue to secretly hurt you?

Girl:

At times, he made me go to church with him and sit next to him. People thought I was such a quiet, devoted daughter. . . Nobody would have believed me. . . . Puppy should have snarled and rushed me. He should have snapped and snapped, and sunk his teeth in my leg. He shouldn't just cowardly slink off behind the pile of bricks, whining, and whimpering—trying to hide like a pathetic coward.

Therapist:

Puppy was a weak coward?

Girl:

No! Puppy was just shocked . . . shocked and confused. A

neighbor came into our yard once and Puppy rushed him and bit him. Puppy was not weak. He was not a coward.

Therapist:

Puppy trusted you?

Girl:

Yes. Yes! Puppy trusted me with his life. I always protected Puppy. I always played with Puppy. I bathed Puppy. I groomed him. I was always kind to Puppy. Puppy learned to trust me not to hurt him. He trusted me to protect him.

Therapist:

And your attack shocked Puppy—confused him?

Girl:

Yes. Puppy didn't even snarl at me anymore. He just whimpered and crouched so pitifully. Then his eyes looked so timid when he tried to slink behind the pile of bricks.

Therapist:

Do you feel you are wicked?

Girl:

What I did was wicked but I needed that adrenalin rush.

Therapist:

You got a rush from hurting Puppy?

Girl:

I get a rush from making any animal suffer—from watching life leave the body. . .. Puppy didn't deserve to die like this though. He trusted me.

Therapist:

Like you trusted your father?

Girl:

Mama doesn't understand. She says I am wicked. She said I am wicked and stained. Maybe she knows I'm not wicked. She might just be hurting. That loathsome, mindless man is her husband—that filthy, nasty, disgusting, heartless bitch!

Please, will you please help me? Help me understand what happened to the nice man who was my father . . . Where did he go? O God, help me, please help me. How could he mess up his little girl like this? How could he?

Therapist:

First you were rubbing your left hand up and down your right arm, then your right hand up and down your left arm. Now, you are vigorously rubbing your hands along your thighs from hips to knee, up and down, up and down.

Girl:

He made me cook for him after all that. He would always make me cook for him. He would sit there and eat . . . He would try to make me eat too—like nothing happened.

Therapist:

He made you cook?

Girl:

He ordered me to cook like I was his maid.

Therapist:

You sat and ate with your father after he forced himself on you?

Girl:

Never! I always locked the toilet door and vomited every time! I should have run outside—run away . . .I should have run out to the road, vomiting . . . I should have run and vomited on his food and let him bash in my head!

Therapist:

You think you would have been better off dead?

Girl:

He bashed up my mind. He should have been more merciful, and just bashed in my skull! No skull, no mind! No protection around mind. Then he could smash mind—smash it, smash it, smash it! Mash it up! Oh God, why didn't he just bash in my brain and kill me dead? Why didn't he? Why didn't he just kick up my head and smash in my skull?

Therapist:

Your father would have been more merciful if he had just smashed your brain like you smashed in Puppy's brain?

Girl:

Suffering ends with death, right? No body, no mind . . . Right? No brain, no mind, no suffering. Right?

Therapist:

You are wondering if death is the end of suffering.

Girl:

O God, help me, help me. Please help me!

Therapist:

You were vigorously rubbing your arms and legs. Now you are tensely bunching up the hem of your skirt with both hands.

Girl:

My mother won't talk to me. She does not understand that he raped me! Every time he violated me! She called me a whore —my own mother called me a whore, my own mother. I miss my mother. She doesn't understand. I was powerless. I did not know what to do so I crawled into a shell when I couldn't stop him. She didn't even notice. I begged her to take me with her whenever she was going out. She always left me with him. I wanted to talk to somebody so badly. I miss my mother.

Therapist:

You miss your mother? You would feel better if your mother would talk with you?

Girl:

My mother does not understand. She never gave me a chance to tell her what happened. She just became a very angry woman. She moved me into my apartment when I came out.

Therapist:

When you came out?

Girl:

Why did I say that? Where did that come from? Something happened between the time I smashed Puppy's head and the time I moved into my apartment. I remember telling my mother I was planning to go to the police about my father because he had robbed me of a treasure. I had become neurotic. My mother snarled at me, and asked if I was crazy. She ordered me to stop talking like a crazy woman. . . . I begged her to listen to my story, but she said I was wicked; that I was a whore.

Therapist:

You have been silent for a while . . .

Girl:

Two of us are here.

Therapist:

Two of you are here?

Girl:

Yes. Two of us are here with you in this session. Mama does not understand. She does not want to understand.

Therapist:

Your mother does not want to understand?

Girl:

He waylaid me . . . He trapped me. Before I could think through what was happening and why it was happening it was already happening. I fought back each time. I whimpered, and whined, and shrieked, and cried. I would run and hide, but each time he would come after me. For almost a whole year I fought back, thinking that Mama would find out and deliver me. Then I gave up. I just gave up. I should not have given up fighting him off. When Mama left to go to her sewing shop, he would hold my hand, lead me to my room and just abuse my body. O God, I never submitted. I always

31

resisted. I wasn't fighting and screaming anymore because I had concluded that any attempt to fight him off was useless. But I always resisted. I loathed him being intimate with me. I loathed the whole disgusting thing. I felt sick sleeping in that room. But I gave up on fighting him off.

Therapist:

You gave up?

Girl:

As soon as he approached me I'd make myself believe I was a little bird on the window sill, looking around at the open space outside, wanting to fly off into the open air, but unable to lift myself off the window sill. After several vain attempts to fly off I would just shrink myself back to an embryo and crawl back into my shell. That was how I was able to survive. That was how she was able to survive—by becoming an embryo again.

Therapist:

She?

Girl:

I told you two of us are here with you in this session.

Therapist:

Two of you are here with me now in this session?

Girl:

Yes. Guess who the other person is.

Therapist:

I should know who the other person is?

Girl:

Yes. You have to know who she is. You have been talking with her all this time.

Therapist:

Why don't you tell me who else is here in this session with us?

Girl:

Look at the name you have on your notepad.

Therapist:

I have the name, Sherry, written here on this notepad.

Girl:

Sherry is a professional woman. She holds an executive position. She's smart, talented, and savvy—always walking erect, with an easy poise. Although she is a pushover in some ways, she is still a very self-confident, efficient, professional woman. She can't be this pathetic, tense, slouching girl here, twisting, and writhing in pain . . . and shame.

Therapist:

The girl you were is still here locked up in the personality of the woman you have become? You were just gripping the hem of your lovely tiered cotton skirt in tight fists. Now, you have ripped your skirt straight up the front . . .

Girl:

I want to be the woman I project but I feel like a pretender. Most of the time I feel like the violated girl—trashy. What he did was wrong! Wrong! Wrong! Wrong! O God, have mercy! That man raped me! He used to be my father, but he raped me! He did not care how much I screamed. He didn't care how frightened I was. He said I was his and he could do what he wants with me! O God, O God, I hate him! I hate him! I hate that Judas! Mama does not know how many times I tried to fight him off. Mama never blamed him. She always blamed me! O God, I hate him. . . .. I hate to see his face; I hate his scent! I feel like puking every time I smell any fragrance that reminds me of him. 1 loathe the man, that nasty betrayer! I hate the image of him in my head! I hate this hate making havoc of my mind!

Therapist:

You have opened your eyes on your own, and you've been sitting up. Go ahead, weep. Weep for your lost innocence. . . . You pulled out a drawing pad . . . You are sketching a . . . a bird . . . a tiny bird . . . in a large hand . . . and a pair of scissors over the bird's wings . . . Another large hand. . . holding the scissors . . . The bird's severed wings are on the window sill. And the bird looks . . . weak and helpless—now it is shrunken into a dark knot. . .. The knot is shrinking. It is an embryo again. It has gone back into its shell— a broken shell. You sketch swiftly and so graphically, like a master artist! Another drawing . . . A tall, elegant woman —smartly dressed . . .In her head is a miniature form of a crouching, weeping girl. . .. What's that unfinished sketch— the miniature form in the head is morphing into the elegant woman?

Girl:

I feel unfinished—incomplete—blocked. Who am I really?

Therapist:

Let the tears flow . . . let them flow. You have been away from your father for many years, but the memory of having been violated by a parent you trusted, hurts . . .

Girl:

In my mind everything feels so recent.

Therapist:

Recall pulls up the distant past to the present.

Girl:

Look at me, I am supposed to be a woman but I'm still the violated girl . . . And it hurts so much. Will it ever stop hurting? O God, have mercy, have mercy on me. God, please, have mercy, and stop this pain. I feel so ashamed—so violated! Will I ever get over this pain and shame?

Therapist:

Your mind is yours to control.

Girl:

What is happening with me? Why am I convulsed in pain? Why am I weeping so much? I was so strong all these years. I don't recall ever weeping this much.

Therapist:

'Seems the little girl is through with hiding. She has come out in the open with conscious recall. To survive all these years, you repressed the pain. You disowned the experience of betrayal by your father. In disowning the experience, you denied yourself the right to grieve for your lost innocence.

Girl:

So this pain ripping through me is grief work?

Therapist:

Yes. Grief work has to be done. But you would be okay. The pain is raw now, but you are okay. The crying will end sometime.

Girl:

I feel like two persons are struggling to coexist in my body?

Therapist:

You had to survive the trauma that distorted you into that betrayed, angry, self-rejecting girl. That young girl is waiting for your acceptance.

Girl:

Part of me is waiting for acceptance?

Therapist:

If you are to feel whole and balanced, you must accept your entire experience. Experience is your teacher. Learn and grow. Living in denial creates inner turmoil. Incest is part of your experience—a distasteful part, but an integral part of your experience. However, you are not your experience. You are what in your mind you choose to be. The beautiful, elegant woman is who you are. Accept her with all her feelings of betrayal, guilt, hurt, and shame. Accept your experience of betrayal, hurt, and shame. Who you now are you always have been. Your father has his own darkness to cope with. You trusted him, but he used and abused your body, apparently with no regard for your mind. His behavior confused, but could not destroy, your mind because your mind was never his to destroy.

Girl:

I feel so confused. I keep thinking that my father must have been bent on destroying me; that he was trying to send me mad by messing up my mind.

Therapist:

You are always in charge of your mind and you did what you had to do to protect your mind. You repressed a segment of memory that back there was too traumatic for you to process. But you are okay.

Girl:

Would I really be okay?

Therapist:

You are okay. You have come out of hiding. Look, you pulled yourself out of reverie.

You are in charge of you. You have consciously taken charge of your mind.

Girl:

How could my mother not be aware of what was happening to me? How could so much be happening to me and my mother not know? Why wasn't she spending more time with me—observing me, listening to me, checking on me? Where was my mother all those hours I would be weeping in silence and pain? She became so aloof. When she should have been hugging me, and helping me get over, she was standing off. She was so cold. I was the one offended, yet she behaved like I offended her. Up till now my mother is unaware of what was happening to me. Now I know why she has been so aloof. Try as I may to please her, she has remained aloof. I've made a slave of myself trying to please my mother.

Therapist:

No need to continue playing weak and helpless; no more need to play the role of people pleaser. You are strong. You don't have to be rejecting the young girl and pushing her on to other people, anymore—not even on to your mother. The young girl is part of your past. She is who you were back there. But you are a woman now. The girl has become a kind, strong, caring, and capable woman.

Girl:

If I am strong, why am I hurting so much, why this gut-wrenching pain? I came for help but I am feeling the worse I've felt in years. Why can't I stop weeping?

Therapist:

For too many years you've been lugging around repressed pain and shame, but you are now in the process of releasing all that shame and pain. This is uprooting time. Your memory has been jangled to shake loose the roots of repressed shame and pain. What was repressed for too long is being uprooted, and is mushrooming on the way out. This is why your pain and shame feels so intense, so overwhelming. But you are okay. Your consciousness has just begun the work of uprooting the lie that you are not a good person, that you are unworthy. In the process you are also shaking the self-defeating language out of your head. This is the final storm before the calm, hence the sudden uncontrollable weeping. "Weeping may endure for a night", as the adage says, "but joy comes in the morning". There is an important task you must eventually take care of, however . . . Here, uses this box of Kleenex . . . a very important task. You have forgiving work to do. But we will get to that in time.

Girl:

Why must everything be about him? How can I think about forgiving him? Why must this be about the one person who has turned my life upside down? What about me? I have to think about me!

Therapist:
This forgiving work is about you.

Girl:
About me forgiving my father? Is this what you are saying?

Therapist:
No, I am not talking about you forgiving your father. This is not about your father. Healing work is about you—you and God. You have been blaming yourself all along, haven't you?

Girl:
Mama was blaming me . . . I did not know what for, but throughout my adulthood I have felt wilted in her presence.

Therapist:
This is not about your mother or your father. This is about you. You might have been echoing what your mother in her frustration said. But it is in your head, not in your mother's, that your thoughts take root. You have been blaming yourself.

Girl:
Coming to think of it, yes, I have been blaming myself. I have been saying to myself that I must be a disappointment why my own mother rejects me. I was saying to myself that I had to make people like me because I evidently wasn't deserving of love. I was saying that I was a bad person. And try as I may, I could not understand the repulsion I felt towards my father, or the repulsion I felt to anything reminding me of him. Do you think my mother would believe I have had no conscious recall of my father raping me over and over again?

Therapist:
You know more than you are consciously aware of. I want your permission to put you in reverie for one more session today.

Girl:
Anything to get me away from blaming myself for

everything. For as long as I've known myself I've been blaming myself even when other people are obviously going out of their way to confront me. This is why I don't even want to talk about forgiving my father. He wronged me, why must I be the one to forgive?

Therapist:

You will find answers to all your questions. For every question your mind throws at you know there is an answer. And you don't have to be afraid to find answers. Now, allow yourself to sink into that armchair. I'll be counting down from ten to one. When I reach one, your eyes will be closed. If for any reason, at any time, you feel uncomfortable and want to get out of reverie, just say stop and I will stop the session. . .. You are at the poolside with your puppy. Who else is there with you?

Girl:

My mother rushes in. She is screaming at me. "What have you done? What have you done? "She screams and screams. I am still holding the bloodied brick in my bloodied hand. My jeans and shirt are splashed with Puppy's blood. I am feeling the thick, sticky blood on my hands and I know it is splashed all over my clothes, and on my face. Puppy's bludgeoned body is a bloody mass of pulverized flesh and broken bones at my feet. I am calm, fearless, and defiant. My mother is agitated. She is wearing a yellow short-sleeve cotton shirt—buttoned down in front, and white knee length shorts. Her toes are manicured with pink nail polish and decorated with daffodil colored flowers.

Her white sandals are designed with daffodil colored cut out floral patterns. Her hair is pulled back in a ponytail. She is flailing her arms and screaming her heart out, as she gazes in horror at the bloody mass at my bloodied feet, but she is not touching Puppy, and she is backing away from me. I'm standing strong and defiant. The scent of Puppy's mangled flesh and blood keeps me on a high. I have just killed and right now, could kill again. I think Mama senses this. Mama goes silent, and I feel an eerie tension over the area. I know our neighbors are outside the wall, listening. Puppy shrieked distressingly before his last whimper. This isn't my first kill. Some neighbors know I've killed before . . .

Therapist:

Some of your neighbors are outside the wall, listening? They know you have killed before?

Girl:

Some. I've stomped the head of birds . . .A few times, cats. Cats are difficult to kill. They raise such a ruckus. My father is holding my mother from behind, and is carefully moving her away from me. She has stopped screaming but she is holding her arms stiff and close to her body, and she is wringing her hands. My fearless eyes are on the both of them. He moves her a safe distance away from me. Now, he dares step towards me, holding out his hand for the brick. He says, "Sherry, give me the brick." I take one powerful step back, jerk back my arm with the brick, and scream, "Don't touch me, you sleaze!"

Therapist:

You have been silent for a long while . . .

Girl:

I'm in the Silence . . . Everything here is silent. White walls and white ceiling. Closed door. Silent nurses in lemon uniforms. Serious nurses in white uniforms. Male doctor in white uniform. Door opens, and door closes. Hands bring medication–tablets, injections. Shifts come and shifts change. But I remain. Night comes and evening goes, but I remain. I am part of the silence.

Therapist:

Any familiar face through all this silence?

Girl:

Just one silent face—my mother's. She knows.

Therapist:

She knows?

Girl:

She knows everything—everything. There is not one thing about my father's abuse that she does not know. She has been in sessions with the psychiatrist and me, sometimes with the Social Worker and me. It's years since I've related to my father. Sometimes I see him from a distance. He walks with a limp. He never looks at me. I can't understand how the loving, caring father of my childhood could have morphed into such a pervert. . ... Why is my mother so angry at me?

Therapist:

You can't make sense of your mother's attitude?

Girl:

Why doesn't she understand? I used to be so afraid of her . . .I heard that chuckle.

Therapist:

Open your eyes. Did you hear what you just said?

Girl:

I used to . . . That was what I said, wasn't it—used to be. I wonder where that came from. I feel different. I feel okay. Everything feels clarified.

Therapist:

Truth does that. Truth clarifies. You still have no idea why your mother is so aloof with you?

Girl:

Wait . . . It is coming back. I exposed the whole nasty mess that day, didn't I? And I screamed at her and blamed her for not protecting me from that blue movies addict—from that filthy man.

Therapist:

Any other memory about that day?

Girl:

I did release that brick, didn't I? And I hit him where it mattered. He bent over, and fell on his back. I was reaching for another brick to finish him off when some neighbors rushed in and held my arms. But I got the bastard. I got the bastard good—just where I wanted to get him—with one smashing blow. The light bulbs are lighting up, one by one.

Therapist:

More bulbs will flicker and glow as you leave here. This is why you must remember . . .

Girl:

Our session tomorrow morning. . .. Yes, I know. My mind would be flooded with memories.

Therapist:

The healing process has begun. You might feel the worse you've felt in your life, but this is part of the healing process. This is the lancing of the boil. And the lancing could feel brutal.

Girl:

What I was running from I now have to face. I know. I also know that everything is alright. Deep within I truly know this. I can regret the past but I can't change it. I can only accept that as painful as recall is what I went through is part of my experience, even the plea of temporary insanity. Mama was embarrassed. I had to go mad to drag the whole disgusting mess out in the open. Now everybody knows. Oh my God, does everybody know?

Therapist:

You know the answer to your question.

Girl:

Yes, everybody knows—my boyfriend knows; the public knows. I've been in denial, walking around with blinders, all these years!

Therapist:

We have much more work to do. We will be working with whatever your mind throws at you—whether in dreams or in wakefulness.

———

End of Part 2, The Girl and Her Therapist

* From Children's Playtime song in *Words of a Caribbean Woman*, (poetry) by the Author.

PART THREE

Releasing the Pain and Shame

RELEASING THE PAIN AND SHAME

In the preceding pages you, as reader, were an invisible observer of the character I call Sherry as she offloaded in therapy sessions. You witnessed her turmoil as she confronted a block of memory she had repressed.

For the sake of all represented by Sherry and for you who might not be aware that you can access the help that Sherry, in desperation, sought, I am including the following additional material as a roadmap to inner peace.

Whatever the cause of your pain or shame, don't ever give in to despair. Relief is closer than you can imagine.

If you feel you just cannot cope with the misery self-loathing, or pain, for whatever reason, is dragging you through, read on and get the help you need.

Inner cleansing is what the following chapters are about, and inner cleansing is spiritual work. Divine power is already yours, but you have to exert your willpower to do your part.

It is in the practice of thinking and behaving differently that you become transformed—that you become the person that is no longer dragged about by what once troubled you.

And here is an important secret I can't wait to share with you —whatever you keep in your mind plays out in your living. So, say positive things to yourself.

Another secret—joy comes to you only as you forgive and practice speaking kindness and love. You will never be at peace as long as you have resentment in your mind.

Get rid of resentment by saying good things about that person you think you hate. Your hate destroys you. You feel revived when you hold thoughts of love and goodness in your mind.

With great love,

Eugenia A. Franklin-Springer
Author
May 2013
USA

"Get this—no matter what is playing out in your life right now, you can at this moment take control of your will, and turn your life in the direction you want to go."   . . . The Author

1 You Matter

Here you are, in a society in which you grew up learning to think a certain way; learning to distinguish between what is right and what is wrong, between what is acceptable and what is unacceptable.

In addition to learning about right and wrong, you also had your own personal standards and values that guided your behavior and helped you to behave responsibly—distinguishing between what you considered acceptable and what you considered unacceptable.

However, something happened that left you feeling like a hypocrite—disappointed in yourself.

You feel guilty of having betrayed your own standards—broken your own moral guidelines, your own rules. Now you just wish the earth would open up and swallow you and your shame.

"One of betrayal's most painful aspects", one author said, "is the cost it takes on your self-esteem".

You feel so devastated. You have been hiding ever since.

I have news for you. You don't have to hide. There is none so flawless that you need to hide from them.

Come out of hiding and let me help you work through those feelings of worthlessness. You can rise from embarrassment, from loss of face, to feel good about yourself again.

2 Hope For You

Once you've been identified as having violated some moral code, or as having been involved in behavior society frowns upon, you tend to feel extremely embarrassed. Even as a victim, you tend to feel so transgressed. You may feel overwhelmed with shame.

And you are usually left on your own to find some way of living with the *shame-fadedness*, with the awareness that there is a question mark about your judgment or worse yet, about your character.

I am here to tell you that you no longer have to struggle on your own and hide because of what happened to you.

You can rise from embarrassment, from *loss of face*, to feel good about yourself again. Yes, you can.

How? The first thing you must do is turn towards yourself. Stop running.

Stop trying to hide.

If it happened to you, as dreadful as the reality might seem, as difficult as it might be to acknowledge what happened, accept that whatever happened is now part of your experience. If it happened to you the experience holds a lesson you must learn.

Learn and grow.

In time, you will examine yourself to understand your feelings. You will reflect on your life in light of this incident. All that is to come.

Right now, however, face the fact that what happened is now part of your experience, and know that in spite of whatever happened, you are still a worthwhile, important person.

3 Why Me?

Why you? Why did this have to happen to you?

Yes, you will ask, why me? You may ask, how could I have allowed myself to sink to such depths of indecency, to such depths of immorality, to such depths of depravity? Or, how could such indecency happen to me?

The answer is simple enough; maybe so simple you may overlook its significance.

Whatever happens to you in this life is for your instruction. There is a lesson you must learn.

Deep inside, you will understand as you quiet your mind, and reflect. Even in writing this, I am asking myself how could a rape, or incest, hold a lesson any one needs to learn?

I confess that I do not have the answer, but you will find the answer because if it happened to you there is a lesson in the whole experience, that you must learn, as you move on to become a stronger person.

God has not abandoned you. It is impossible for you to abandon yourself. The Spirit within is your guide. God within is your guide. You were born to live—to live gloriously.

Every confrontation with yourself challenges you to step up and be stronger.

And you are not alone. Many others are struggling through situations like this one you are emerging from.

Who knows, something you have learned, or are learning, may equip you to help somebody out here—somebody no one but you might be able to reach.

4 Face Your Distress

Somebody violated you. Along the way that person will meet with consequences Leave them to their consequences. You take care of yourself.

Where you go from here must not be about them, but about you. You attend to your healing and growth.

When someone overpowers you emotionally, physically, or otherwise, they momentarily take control of your power. Now that you are back in control of your body, stay in control of your mind and refuse to give any more of your focus or power to the violator.

Your mind is the seat of your power. Think strength and you will manifest strength.

You are intrinsically important. You are naturally a beautiful soul. Nothing done to you can diminish your intrinsic worth.

5 Responsible For Self

Living is about choreographing your life story. And you are each moment caught up in portraying your story.

You alone are in control of your soul.

God in you—that spirit of yours—watches over your soul and enables you to rise above every attack, against every assault, and move on in strength.

You have the final say to how you would respond to any life event.

History uses the term, "heroes" for those who despite brutal assaults on their body, stay in control of their mind and their soul.

Nelson Mandela, Harriet Tubman, Sojourner Truth, Elie Wiesel, Oprah Winfrey, Maya Angelou are among our heroes. They are also our role models.

These men and women could have stayed broken in spirit because of the assaults on their body and their mind, but though their body was attacked no oppressor was allowed control over their mind or over their soul. Because they stayed in control of their mind and soul they are today internationally perceived as luminaries.

What matters is that you now take full responsibility for deciding where you go from wherever you find yourself.

WakeUp Call

If you have violated your own standards and values, and crossed the line of respect, but now regret what you did, and want to live right from here on, confront your past with courage.

If you are still struggling to cope with memories of what happened to you in the past, confront that past with courage.

You cannot change the past,

Whatever has left you feeling badly or even ashamed was a wake-up call. Wake up and take control of your life. Waste no more time wallowing in guilt, regret, shame, or self-pity.

From here on prove to yourself that despite the bitterness of past experiences you can come to terms with your past and move on with your life.

As sad as your experience might have been, what you did, or what happened to you, can never diminish your worth. Your worth is intrinsic.

Of course you could be feeling badly about what others might think about you, or even about what some might be saying about you. Reason would tell you that you can't do a thing about what others think or say.

What if you feel you have brought shame on yourself by poor choices? Again, where you go from here is completely up to you. How you use your mind from here on could signal *a turning point* in your life.

In the next chapter we talk about that *turning point.*

7 Turning Point

You will be focusing on your own thinking rather than on what others think about you. Your mind controls your living, so if you want to change the quality of your living you must change the way you have been thinking—the habitual thoughts mulled over in your mind.

Since your thoughts are constantly creating your reality, you must examine your mind to see what thoughts have been holding you down in pain and shame. When you identify those thoughts you must let them go—replace them with happy thoughts.

I am about to lead you into confronting yourself. Know this, the reason you do what you do is always your decision and your responsibility. The reason you have been in pain, and tortured with shame is because you are not recognizing your intrinsic worth and the power of your thoughts and consequently the power of every word you speak.

Word is power. You are in pain because you feel like a victim. And naturally, if you feel like a victim, you would be blaming somebody —the victimizer. You are in shame because you feel belittled— diminished. You are feeling like you just can't cope with what you think of yourself. You feel extremely uncomfortable with yourself.

This is your problem right here—how you feel about yourself because of what you have been telling yourself about yourself.

You are about to turn your entire life experience around as you realize two things:

        (1) that you alone have created the kind of life
           you are living right now; and

        (2) that you definitely have the power to create
           for yourself the peaceful life you so
           greatly desire.

Now you are about to examine your story. You will be looking at your mind to understand the dynamics behind the pain and shame you have been putting yourself through.

8 Know Yourself

You shall know the truth and the truth shall set you free. Know the truth about yourself.

Get a large writing pad, and a couple pens. You will need these soon. Also, stay close to a mirror.

This exercise is about taking responsibility for the pain you struggle with and the shame that threatens to overwhelm you. It is okay. Just you and your memory here now. You are safe at this moment. No need to be defensive. No need to hide and cringe from your memory.

You don't have to be afraid of your memory. You are asked to write your story, but read through this chapter first, then go aside by yourself and write. Give yourself at least a couple hours free of interruption.

Think. Why the pain and the shame?

Confront the feelings you've been carrying around in your mind. Let them surface.

Regardless of the duration of time these feelings have been with you, you are about to throw them off. First, however, these feelings must surface.

Because, better than anyone else, **you** know your thoughts and your feelings, you must tell yourself your story. Listen, and pay attention to what you have been telling yourself all this time—perhaps unconsciously. Write it out. Write your story.

The pain, the self-recriminations, the anger, the hate, the bitterness, the rage—look at all that stuff in your mind. Write it out.

Listen to what you have been saying to yourself in your mind when you feel ashamed. Listen to what you have been telling yourself in your mind when you suffer as you recall your past. Write out the conversation between you and yourself.

Feel your feelings. Listen intently to what your feelings are saying. Feel how your feelings wrap themselves around the tone of your voice; feel how your deep pain mutates into anger, then rage. Listen to the emotions that so often feel as though they are locking you down. Think of how those emotions pelt out through your tone of voice and body language to jettison others away from your company, to jettison others away from the venom distorting your identity— misrepresenting your beautiful self—your hurting self.

You might be able to camouflage the hurt and pain that fuels your anger when you just don't want to deal with all those repressed feelings. But this exercise is about dealing with those repressed feelings; so get aside by yourself, where you can be alone for at least a couple hours. Grab your pen and writing paper.

You are going to be looking at what is coming out from inside you. Once and for all you are going to identify where your inner distress is coming from.

To clear and re-energize your mind, take seven deep breaths while holding your spine ram-rod straight and your head erect. Repressed emotions not only impact on your communication, they also distort your energies and therefore distress your tissues. Deep breathing cleanses and re-energizes your tissues.

Now, stand in front a mirror. Smile with yourself. Consciously relax.

How are you feeling? Feel the feelings in your body. Gaze at your forehead, Is it feeling relaxed? Your facial muscles—your eyes, your mouth, your lips—how are they feeling? Smile, and feel the difference in these head muscles as you smile. Gaze at your throat. Relax your neck. Next, your chest. Gradually go down your body, down to your toes. Relax every part.

Take a couple deep breaths again.

Sit in a comfortable position. Reflect, how have you been feeling, deep inside. What distresses you? How are you feeling about yourself? What do you feel guilty about? Have you been feeling like a hypocrite?

Why? Are there some persons you want to stay far from? Why? Any one you really hate? Why? What thoughts have you feeling so ashamed? What secret you are holding that is tearing you apart? Why are you keeping this a secret? Something you did in the past that is haunting you? Why?

This exercise is only about you.

You are going to write it all out. And you must take as long as you want. Forget about spelling and grammatical errors.

Just spill your feelings onto paper. What are you blaming yourself for? What are you saying to yourself that is keeping you in all this distress?

No going back to edit. Let emotions grab hold of any word available in your vocabulary at the moment to express your feelings.

Spill out the conversations always going on in your head. Write it out.

Yes, this is a painful assignment. This is akin to trying to stare smack into the center of the fiery setting sun. But once you, taking necessary safety precautions, keep your eyes steady on the glaring sun, going past the blinding rays, your eyes rest gently on a soft, soothing, elliptical orb—no more blinding rays.

Get home to yourself, past the blinding, scorching self-disappointment, past the self-defensive posturing, past the soul searing struggle to be counted as someone more important than you think they think you are.

You are important, regardless of the details of your past. You, yourself, are important. And you have only to convince yourself of your intrinsic worth, regardless of stories about you. You do not have to convince any other of your worth.

Many, for various reasons are suffering as much as you are suffering. Many of us who seem more self-assured now, have suffered as you are suffering.

The fact that many of us have overcome—have come through—must tell you that there's hope for you.

Truthfulness will always set your mind at ease because Truth always sits comfortably with your conscience, and makes you feel good about yourself.

Now, you are about being truthful with yourself. Your truth is in what you have been telling yourself, and how what you have been telling yourself has been affecting your feelings. So write out your distress, Why do you feel embarrassed. What really is at the root of that anger; what are the games you play, to be counted out here?

Write! Write out your story. This is between you and yourself. This is about you expressing yourself to yourself.

9 Meet Self-image

Well, you have confronted yourself either in writing or with the aid of an electronic recording device.

Since you live with what you think of yourself, it is important that you know what you think of yourself.

Your view of everybody and everything is influenced by how you feel about yourself. How you relate to others—how you live—has everything to do with what you tell yourself about yourself.

You live with your self-image. The key to successful living is knowing yourself; therefore, the work you were asked to do in the preceding chapter is very important. You must not put it off till another time, and you must not skip it.

Read what you have written, or listen to what you have recorded. Allow yourself to become aware of how you think, of how you feel, of the rules and values that determine how you present yourself.

How are you feeling now that you have taken the time to know more about yourself?

Initially, it could be difficult to read what you have written, or listen to what you have recorded. But the discomfort eases with repetition.

Read it again. Play the recording again. Repeat this for as many times as it takes to remove the sting from this confrontation with yourself.

It might take days, or weeks, to pull the sting out of this self-confrontation. But the pain eases and then goes away completely as you repetitively consciously affirm your intrinsic worth and with that reassurance, recall in detail whatever experience you have been feeling so badly about.

If you need help, go to a psychotherapist, or Family Life Counselor. These persons can lead you deeper into self-understanding.

If recalling seems more than you feel you can cope with right now, see a Mental health therapist. The Psychiatrist is there to help you with mental health issues. The Social Worker is trained to help with matters like yours.

You do not have to feel embarrassed or ashamed to tell your story. All of us who have been helping people sort out their thinking, are acquainted with stories like yours. Some of us have had stories like yours.

Accept yourself as a valuable, lovable, adequate human being who was involved in situations you would not deliberately choose to be involved in ever again.

The past is past. It is gone, and there is nothing you can do about it. This moment, however, is fresh and new. You could build beautiful thoughts now.

And what if you were the violator? If you were the victimizer, then you must confront what you did.

Face it. Do not make excuses for yourself. Acknowledge that you did wrong, and consciously, actively, forgive yourself.

You have the power of mastery over your body. And you have the power and fortitude to harness the energies of your mind, body, and soul so the Spirit in you could guide you into creating the kind of life you desire.

Now, put away your paper (or recording) in a safe place so you could read it again before destroying it if you don't want other eyes to read what you have written, or other ears to hear what you have recorded. Personally, I like to keep whatever I write or record, for self-assessment later down the road. And though when younger, I cringed in embarrassment at the mere thought of other eyes falling on what I had written, now it doesn't matter as much whose eyes see my soul spillage.

Writing or recording the truth about how you feel, and what you have been habitually saying about yourself, allows you to be more aware of how you had been creating your misery.

In looking at yourself you become aware not only of whatever is playing on your mind but also of your inner and outer response. You become the observant little bird on your own shoulder, watching closely your moment to moment inner response to all that is happening about you and within you.

If pain and shame have been for too long your constant companion, you have been living in misery. Now, let misery be a wake-up call.

Misery is a state in which you have been thrashing about emotionally, desperate to escape to feeling balanced again.

In misery, memory could feel like a merciless avenger until you quiet yourself and realize that you don't know how to escape the self-loathing, the pain, the shame, the self-doubt, the feelings of non-accomplishment—you don't know how to live a self-validating life. This is the essence of misery.

In misery you come to realize your need for help. As in desperation you cry out for help, Spirit within lifts your consciousness to greater awareness of what your life is about. This is how your unspoken cry for deliverance is answered—Spirit allows you to get a glimpse of the tremendous and grand possibilities before you.

1O   New Language

A basic requirement for happiness is self-acceptance.

You must do the preparatory work if you are to replace shame with self-acceptance.

Self-acceptance is about being bubbly happy deep in your soul. It is the inner proclamation that you are okay.

Regardless of what you went through or what you did, you are now, in this moment, okay, and you can choose to live from here on as one who is okay.

To get to the place of self-acceptance, you start by consciously staying in control of your self-talk.

Make it a habit to speak strength to yourself— "I am strong, thank you, God; I am adequate, thank you, God; I am important, thank you, God".

Word is power.

The spoken word reinforces its messages in your mind.

Affirm your power; affirm your self-worth. Make a habit of speaking strength to yourself.

No more waste of energy with self-pity, or hostility.

You are strong. Thank God for strength. What you are feeling is about how you are thinking.

Accept responsibility for how you feel. How you feel could never ever be another person's responsibility, even if that person deliberately tries to provoke you.

This is why it is so useless to have confrontations with other persons because of how you think they made you feel. Regardless of what another says or does, you alone are responsible for your response.

Take time throughout your waking moments to praise God, love yourself, and demonstrate honor to yourself and others.

You have to make yourself be what you want to be. You have to close the gap between how you are and how you know you ought to be.

Whether you are feeling guilty because of something you did, allowed, or instigated, or because you resisted another throwing a guilt trip at you, or because you thought you were helpless but now realize you were not—regardless of your rationale back there for having opened your mind to guilt feelings, it's time to release that poison, and the resentment it keeps splattering inside you.

Waste no more time hiding in shame and guilt.

You are capable of straightening out your mind, correcting your thinking, changing your behavior, and walking strong from here on.

The language of self-acceptance must now be part of your new thinking.

1

1 End the Guilt-Tripping

To get to the place of self-acceptance, you have to get off the guilt trip.

If you are on a guilt trip because you deviated from your own standard for right conduct, you could work through that guilt, but if you are feeling guilty because you refuse to give in to another's attempt to control and manage your life, you have no need to feel guilty; you have done no wrong.

Sexual offenders, and other violators of another's personal boundaries, trigger off mental confusion in the person they assault, often leaving the victim feeling responsible for what happened. This false guilt can create problems throughout the victim's life.

Every person—including children—has their own moral values—their own, perhaps unspoken, non-verbalized rules of conduct to guide their living.

These rules are reflections of their moral values. Even the child knows when their moral values have been compromised.

Sometimes the offended feels guilty, wondering if they in any way was responsible for the assault against them. Theirs is false guilt. The guilt of the offender, the one who committed the act of violation, is true guilt.

Guilt, true guilt, is torture. And anyone who has violated their own personal code of conduct knows true guilt. But to the mind that does not understand false guilt and how to get rid of it, the self-blame and self-loathing can sear as brutally as true guilt.

If you have violated, and your guilt leads to remorse, for you there is hope—redemption, even.

Like the person burdened with false guilt you don't have to forever live with guilt and shame.

12 About False Guilt

A word about guilt! True guilt is that distressing tension you feel when you violate your own moral code—those values, standards, and rules that buttress your character and inform your conscience—leaving no question in your mind about what is right and what is wrong.

True guilt can lead to remorse, and remorse can prod you back into living true to your moral values, in line with your personal rules.

False guilt is the conscience-whipping, inner distress you endure when old disabling beliefs of personal inadequacy are allowed to play havoc with your thinking, leaving you feeling irrationally guilty and shamefacedly responsible for whatever is not working out well.

False guilt is sometimes used to control.

Manipulating persons could try to pressure you by making you feel guilty for not going along with their agenda.

Even as you resist giving in to manipulators, however, they might accuse you of being the cause of their devious behavior, or even the cause of outcomes completely out of your control. They might dredge up instances from your past, even make up stories, or twist the truth to make you feel badly. All part of their agenda to bend or break you so you would give in to whatever they are demanding of you.

Observe however that persons of integrity never try to make any feel guilty—never try to manipulate. Also, no one who is at peace with herself or himself ever tries to make another feel badly.

False guilt can in so many ways ensnare the unsuspecting.

A child who regardless of honor and respect for the elders, resists the sexual advances of a parent or parenting person, or who refuses to go against conscience regardless of pressure from a parent or other trusted individual, could feel guilty and conflicted for not honoring the adult, or for whatever blame is heaped on him or her by a manipulating victimizer.

A parishioner could feel conflicted, confused, and even guilty, when confronted with the advances of a revered but randy religious leader.

A patient could feel guilty and embarrassed by the personal intimate interest displayed by an unethical medical practitioner.

A vulnerable, emotionally conflicted client could be confused by the intimate advances, maybe even fondling, of a horny mental health therapist.

Victims are well acquainted with the guilt-generating questions, "Did I encourage this? Did I bring this on?"

Manipulators thrive on generating confusion and false guilt.

While you are turning away from past indiscretions and past behaviors that might have caused others pain, some might be still struggling to overcome the emotional or mental wounds your behavior might have caused. Despite all your apologies and attempts to heal old wounds, some might still be blaming you.

So, can you stop them from talking about you? I don't think so. Should you allow yourself to be distraught because others, perhaps with just cause, might be talking about you?

All you can do is work on your self-acceptance, and send a blessing in the direction of your accusers.

Talk to your conscience and refuse to feel guilty when you have done nothing to feel guilty about, or when you have forgiven yourself and even apologized for past lapses some are still throwing at you.

If your conscience is scorching you because you feel you could have avoided what happened, accept that at the time that was where you were, feeling helpless, trapped, or vulnerable, for whatever reason. Now, you are more aware of the power of your resolve.

Practice asking God for guidance, and watch how your peace would increase, and fear decrease.

Live an open life, holding secrets for none, and having none hold secrets for you. Fearlessly, own up to whatever you have done.

This way you leave no room for any 'attack and avoid' game with those out to distress.

"*To thine own self be true, then it must follow as the night the day that thou canst not then be false to any man.*" William Shakespeare.

Stay in conscious control of your mind.

Refuse to be swayed by any attempt of others to burden you with false guilt when you know you have done nothing to feel guilty about.

"Joyful living is your birthright, but to access this much available gift, you have to cultivate a moment to moment waking relationship with God; you must allow yourself to experience God as a constant companion, one with whom you are always dialoguing." . . . The Author

13 Peace IN Submission

How can you go from a mind wracked with pain and shame, to a mind at peace?

You have to reprogram your mind. You start by acknowledging that there has to be a power that enables you to be—to live. Attune your mind to that power and you will be guided into peaceful living.

You and I—humans--are co-creators with this Infinite Power some of us call God. God in you has programmed you to control your body and your experiences. You do this through your thoughts and words.

Through your words you are equipped to speak peace and harmony into your living.

You have the power.

From here on your life can be heaven on earth. How can you accomplish the turn around? Affirm your joy, affirm your power, affirm your health. Fill your mind with the word messages of what you want to be true for you.

"I am joy. I am peace. I am strong. I am power. I am health."

These messages rightly describe your birthright. You have learned otherwise and so through your past you had been behaving as one who was so weak you became a victim; one who was so unworthy you lived in distress. What your mind affirmed was reflected back to you in the quality of your living.

Now you are submitting your mind to the Infinite Source of peace.

And you are speaking peace, and joy, harmony, and health, wealth, and strength into your living.

The Eternal spirit in you is working in you bringing your living into alignment with your affirmations.

Be calm; be still. You will be guided to do what you must do.

All that is required of you is complete submission. You have to submit your will to God. The mind that is in complete submission to the Spirit within will uncover its own inner peace.

"... If you have violated, and your guilt leads to remorse, for you there is hope—redemption, even." . . . The Author

1⁴ New Mindset

Your past might not be what you now wish it was. But you can do nothing about that. What you can do is take control of your life from here on.

Aware now that your word is power and that your mind is constantly controlling the quality of your living, you must now boldly exercise mastery over your life. With your mind centered on the Eternal Source—on God, begin now to take responsibility for managing your life.

What does this mean? What do you have to do? Start by acknowledging the Almighty, 'the Unchanging All-knowing' that sustains all, as the only Power.

Next, speak only words that build,

"God Almighty is the only power. I am the temple of God Almighty. Where I am Omnipotence is; where I am Omniscience is; where I am Omnipresence is."

Let your mind dwell on the marvels of nature—on the beauty and on the intricacies of life. Think of the miracle of your own life—of how your body is sustained with a blood circulatory system, a respiratory system, and all the other biological systems that from birthday to birthday sustain life in you.

Think of the miracle of the life-sustaining air, of the miracle behind every sprouting seed, of the precision of heavenly bodies.

Contemplate and give praise to the eternal power that keeps you in the midst of all this. If instead of worry and fret your mind is now occupied with acknowledging the beauty of nature, and appreciating the miracle of your own existence, your mind has passed a turning point. It is now in a 'praise' mode, a mode that supports celebration, not distress.

Keep a song in your heart—a song of affirmation of that which is beautiful.

"God is my life; God is my strength; God is my sustenance; I am strong, I am health, I am harmony. Everything I need is supplied; praise and thanks to the holy name; the Eternal is my strength and my fortress, praise and glory."

With such words of praise and affirmations you will be resetting your mind.

As you yield your efforts to living at a higher level, the spirit in you—God in you—will continuously guide. Be alert. Spend time in the silence thinking about God, and watch and see what happens.

With your new mindset you will be more compassionate to others, even to those who criticize you. You won't be prone to take offense, rather, you would examine the criticism and see if it contains some message you need to attend to. Critics can sometimes be great teachers.

In the old mindset you might have been the ticking bomb ready to explode whenever somebody got you vexed or things did not work out as you expected. Now you can use your mind in support of peaceful living.

Whenever you sense a feeling of annoyance creeping up on you, say, as author Ken Keyes suggests in his book, *A Conscious Person's Guide to Relationships,* "What would happen if even though I would have preferred things to be different, I refuse to upset myself if they are not?"

And you don't upset yourself because you accept full responsibility for your peace of mind. You are working with your affirmations. You know you are a valuable, important, worthwhile human being. Further, you know that nothing and no one outside there holds the key to your peace.

Your wellbeing is intrinsic. Nothing said or done is a threat to your control center—your mind.

The only way what happens out there could threaten you is if you feel like you are intrinsically not good enough—a 'no-good'—and you would defend with your life any move to show you up like a nobody.

People who are aware that they are intrinsically good enough don't take umbrage when another disagrees with them. They can differentiate between attacking the problem and attacking the person.

As you habitually practice this change in self-talk, your mind is being reprogrammed.

You learn to allow what you can do nothing about, and live joyfully in the moment.

You can't change the past. You can change only your self-talk, and in changing your self-talk you guarantee for yourself a change of feelings, and therefore a change of experience.

Habitual self-talk sinks its implications into your subconscious— from where your behavior is managed.

This is how it is with any message oft repeated. So, for example, let's say somebody abused you, leaving you convinced that something is wrong with you, if you don't challenge that feeling that something is wrong with you, in time your self-talk will be highlighting that feeling.

The implications of your self-talk find an anchor in your subconscious, and from there influence your living.

Regardless of your experience, a sunny, positive disposition paves the way for a brighter reality.

Right now you have within you the Inner Guide taking you through the change process.

You are not alone.

It seems that when you are feeling the worst, God in you is right there for you. But you have work to do—work that only you can do.

You have to stop encouraging the flow of negative thoughts.

EUGENIA A. FRANKLIN-SPRINGER PH.D.

For your own benefit, make yourself say words of thankfulness and praise.

Refuse to utter one word of discouragement; refuse to send verbal or nonverbal messages that distress.

Change starts with your silent acknowledgement that God is the only power, and your affirmation that where you are, God is.

Repeat silently or audibly words of positive affirmations: "Thank you, God of Love for the awareness that I am lovable; I am clean; I am pure; I am strong; I am adequate; I am capable; I am courageous; I am somebody; I am important; I am good enough, thank you, Eternal, Loving God.

"They may have transgressed my body, but they have no access to my soul, Power Divine.

"I have done some unclean acts, but I acknowledge that I am intrinsically pure and whole. From here on I am living out of my purity and wholeness".

With every breath give thanks and praise to the holy name, even as you ask for guidance.

Apart from speaking words of truth to yourself, you must be consciously aware of how you present yourself.

If you have been behaving like a victim, you need to start this moment adopting the behavior of an overcomer. Create the reality you desire.

If you have been oppressing another, repent, and from this moment, respect everyone as you would wish to be respected.

Your problem is not what happened, but the state of your mind right now. And though you cannot change what has already happened, you can change the state of your mind; you can reprogram your mind.

Word is power.

Audibly or silently use words that strengthen. And let your

behavior be congruent with your words.

But beyond your use of verbal affirmations must be your manifested change in behavior. Right now, make yourself turn the corner. Do things differently.

Change comes when thinking differently powers a change in how you do things.

1 5 Beyond Guilt

Forgive yourself for having given in to your humanity; for not having behaved perfectly. Forgive yourself for having felt afraid and weak.

And if you were a perpetrator, forgive yourself, only if you are remorseful, for having arrogantly and crassly crossed the line and taken from another what was not yours to take, or for transgressing another's line of respect to inflict hurt and trauma.

If you are looking for a way out from under the load of shame and guilt you have to stop the guilt talk. Right now, stop the defensiveness.

Stop the self-excusing language. Talk through to yourself what you did. Talk through what you believe was done to you.

Tell yourself how you feel about yourself. Say the words aloud so you hear yourself. You should have done this in the exercise in Chapter Eight.

If you were a perpetrator, seek no hiding place—make no excuses.

You were also molested, abused in childhood? This is no excuse for you to have transgressed another.

Those who are not aware of their inherent strength, seek out hiding places where they can be sheltered from the glare of self-examination, from the pain of self-confrontation.

You are strong. Make yourself look at what you did. Go back and read what you wrote in Chapter Eight. If you did not do the assignment, I suggest that you stop now and do it.

Confront yourself.

You are responsible for what you did to another. Seek no sympathy. Look to no one for compassion. Accept the harsh truth that you wronged another.

Only in facing the harsh truth would you be ready for self-forgiveness, with which comes freedom from shame and guilt.

And what if you were just a child, or a young person when you were interfered with, abused, or when you were involved in whatever has left you with this shame, how do you deal with the guilt now? Why do you feel so guilty?

I believe the guilt comes from a deep awareness, well crystallized even in early childhood, that responsibility for your life is with you; that regardless of age, you are expected to be responsible for yourself; that you must never relinquish responsibility to another, not even to an abuser; that your will must always be strong; and you must always do right.

At what age does the child feel responsible for actions done?

I don't know. I suppose it depends on parenting—on what the mind learned. What I know is that some adults are battling shame and guilt for what they did or what was done to them at age three or even younger.

Could it be that at a very early age the child has already formulated some concept of personal responsibility, some concept of what constitutes good and bad behavior?

In learning values does the child learn to be self-condemning?

Regardless of your story, accept responsibility for your healing. Go over the scenario you have been running from, in your mind.

The shame and embarrassment is not in what happened. The shame and pain is in your judgment and condemnation of yourself—in your self-talk. Change your self-talk.

Acknowledge your responsibility for what you were involved in. Go over the scenario in your mind. Face it.

Accept that this is part of your story. And your story is part of the human story. No matter how devastated you feel facing your story, make yourself look at it.

When you can look yourself in the eye without flinching you would be able to look in the eye of any other without flinching.

"To thine own self be true, then it must follow as the night the day that thou cannot then be false to any man."

You alone can pursue your healing. You alone determine how your past will affect your present.

Within you is the power that takes you beyond the picture that once filled your mind with shame and self-loathing.

But you have to look at that picture till looking at it causes you no pain, no shame. You have to look at it while knowing you are no longer there.

I don't think you can do this in your own strength. God in you brings you to the place of self-acceptance.

Be patient with yourself. Stay in prayer and right conduct if you want to flee shame and be infused with peace.

If you have not done the exercise in Chapter Eight because right now you can't look at your past, okay, leave it alone. At the right time you will get back to it. By then looking at it might not be so difficult.

1⁶ As Creator

Conscious affirmations are positive messages you repeatedly say to yourself. Repeat affirmations of your worth: "I am somebody special; I am strong; I am on the path of success; whatever I choose to complete, I complete; I am in control of my will-power; God is my guide; God is my strength; everything in my life is working harmoniously".

Why should you repeat these affirmations? So their messages would sink into your subconscious and shape the way you think, and therefore shape your outcomes.

You are always making affirmations. Now you are making them consciously. You are no longer drifting through life, passively, controlled by a vague sense of who you are or what your life is about.

You are no longer leaving your mind carelessly exposed to whatever messages others throw out there in talk or songs.

You are awake and walking consciously. No longer are you allowing feelings about how others treated you or what others are doing to you, to control you. You are about taking active control of your life.

"I don't like what happened; I don't like what I did; I wish I wasn't part of any of this, but what is, is, and in all this I am responsible for me and for my conduct.

"I ask the Divine to guide me from here on, so I could learn what each experience is meant to teach, and in the process manifest peace, joy, and right conduct.

"From here on, I will speak only words that uplift and heal—no foolish, hurtful, empty, boasting, or self-pitying words; I will behave with integrity; I will act with prudence."

One more thing—know that nothing happens by chance. There is a reason for everything. Your life is working, according to a plan—your plan.

This exercise about self-confrontation and affirmations allows you to be aware of how you have been unconsciously, perhaps, creating your experiences, and how you can now consciously, create the life you desire.

Stewing yourself in guilt and shame robs you of the opportunity to focus on how you created your past. Guilt talk and blame talk, like any other sour or fretful expressions, throw you back in the old mindset.

Even what seems to have been a horrible experience, holds for you some important life lesson you must learn so you won't have to go through such an experience again.

Keep an eye open for the lessons life is minute by minute presenting. And examine your self-talk and behavior to be aware of what you are doing to attract, or create these experiences.

To grow and progress, you must look into each experience to learn what it is teaching you—not what it is teaching the other person, but what it is teaching you.

From here on, you can avoid creating more painful experiences, even as you learn from those you have created.

The inability to benefit from an experience robs you of the opportunity to grow.

This is one reason why resentment is so poisonous.

The resentful response consumes your consciousness so that all you see is how the other person is so wrong.

As a resentful person, your emotional response cannot accommodate reflection and self-examination.

When burdened with resentment, facing self feels too devastating because you still have self-acceptance and self-forgiving work to do.

The resentful response is rooted in guilt and shame, and cannot afford self-examination, so it is fired with anger and sulking, and a draining of vigor.

In releasing the pain and shame, resentment has to be released. It is poisoning only you who are harboring it, no one else—except perhaps those who have to share your space.

So let go your resentment by affirming your worth, and behaving lovingly and kindly to all.

You are lovely and worthy of happiness, so right now, affirm your worth, and be happy.

"What you have been saying to yourself has you where you are, accounts for how you feel, and influences the quality of communication you have with others." ... The Author

17 Addressing Abusers

If despite all you have been reading, you still feel burdened with guilt and shame because you were an abuser, I am here talking to you. You also can offload your guilt and pain. But first you must confront your past.

You must look wide-eyed at what you did, and accept full responsibility for every trauma inflicted by you.

Maybe you haven't till now, thought of yourself as an abuser, but let's do some reflecting.

Have you—including you (or we) who in a parenting role mercilessly punished your (our) children, tormented, provoked, or tortured them mentally or emotionally, or neglected them altogether —brought trauma to another? Without shrinking, we who are guilty must accept full responsibility for what we did—make no excuses.

Better it is to face the glare of your (our) imperfection by acknowledging what you(we) know is the truth, than to indulge in cowardly behavior, afraid to acknowledge that at some time in the past you(we) were abusive.

Accept the truth about yourself—have you terrorized, threatened, sexually enslaved, or in any other way traumatized another? Did you cross the line of respect by displaying inappropriate behavior?

If you are even now pointing the finger of blame at someone you know is guilty of the above transgressions, how about some introspection?

Often, shame with its crippling feelings of personal inadequacy, and self-condemnation, hides behind the finger of blame.

"We have to stand erect in that place of utter humiliation and know our intrinsic worth. We are held in that place of utter humiliation till shame with its load of fear is melted away, and we learn that our worth is neither in things without, nor in anyone's perception of our worth . . ." from *The Spiritual Journey.*

Have you committed a crime to which you have not yet confessed, or for which you have not yet made restitution?

The mind is all we have to guide us through life. We must make peace with our mind—must make peace with our self, if we are to be free of pain and shame.

Let me specifically address the issue of sexual abuse. Too many are suffering under a shroud of secret shame because they were interfered with, or because they did the interfering.

This publication is about releasing the shame and with it, the pain. So, let's do some self-confrontation.

Did you feel strong sexual attraction to a child, or to an adult who had no such interest in you, and did not consent to consensual intimacy?

There's no transgression in feeling. Feelings come and feelings go.

Your responsibility is to stay with right conduct regardless of feelings, so I put the question to you, did you reach out to touch that person? Did you force yourself on the person?

It is a criminal act for an adult to interact sexually with a child whether or not that child is a willing partner.

Urges to be sexually inappropriate, must never be indulged but rather, must be ignored. Unreinforced, they go away.

I am not trying to minimize the power of sexual urges, just as I am not trying to minimize the God given right of everyone to have their personal boundaries, their line of respect, respected by you regardless of your horniness.

Strength of temptation is no excuse for yielding.

Are you guilty of having sexually molested, or abused another?

Since we are talking specifically about releasing the shame of having been sexually molested, I put the question even more directly to you—did you, as a grandparent or older relative, touch that child inappropriately, even just once? Did you make a sex slave of a child who trusted you?

Did you as a parent touch your child, or release your sexual passion on the body (and consequently the mind) of your child, even once? Did you make a sexual partner of your child?

If you did you need to apologize for having confused the child's mind, and you must desist from any such behavior in the future.

Further, you need to seek professional advice about how to go about mitigating the effect of your indiscretion, so you could, if possible, save your child from a life of turmoil, and learn how to redirect your mind so you would never again be guilty of such indiscretion.

Did you as an uncle, or aunt, cousin, or close family friend, trusted caretaker, or trusted associate, fellow student, or roommate, employer, or even as a neighbor, cross that line of trust, and release your sexual passion on another, either through touching or engaging in any other type of sexual behavior—even in lascivious communication?

Did you as a member of the clergy, or as an educator, cross the line of integrity and trust, and indulge in sexual behavior, or sex talk with any under your care?

Did you take advantage of that person who went to you to unburden their soul—did you reach out to them for inappropriate intimacy?

Did you as a professional to whom the public turns for help with their mental confusion, cross the line and fondle that person you should have been helping?

Did you even go beyond fondling?

Did you violate another who did not give their consent to be intimate with you?

Did you have, or do you now have, your child sexually enslaved?

What I am addressing here is for you who harbor some measure of shame for your violation of another.

If you have habitually violated the trust of those who trusted you, "your heart might be hardened"; you might no longer feel shame—that inner indicator that signals a need to change your ways. But for your sake and for the sake of others who may cross paths with you, I pray that you also would change your ways and desist from contributing to the emotional confusion of any other.

But back to you whose inner comfort is being eaten away by shame.

The shame you feel for having lusted, you could deal with in your head. Thoughts come to us unbidden. Even if you indulge in fantasy, you could pull your mind back to living safe. But acting on your fantasies to force yourself onto another is crossing the line.

Apart from owing the victim restitution, you have committed a crime for which you also need to make restitution to yourself.

It is up to you to determine if thoughts of transgressing another—sexually, criminally, or otherwise—are becoming so powerful you need help to defuse them.

But if you crossed the line and forced your desire to have your sexual needs met through the use of another's body, you should feel guilty.

You are guilty of gross misconduct. Yours is true guilt.

The load of guilt the victim lugs around and suffers under could be false guilt.

You—therapist, molester, abuser, libidinous professional, ruttish cleric—are guilty of gross misconduct. Harsh labels? Harsher is the trauma inflicted on the person you made your victim.

Accept the raw ugliness of which you are guilty—the raw ugliness of what you have done to the victim and to yourself.

You stole—you took what was not yours—maybe nothing material, but something way more valuable, an individual's sense of personal reverence, their sense of propriety, their right to have their personal boundaries respected.

Accept the ugly reality that you made yourself a thief—maybe not caught, but still a thief.

To get past this blotch in your life, you must accept the harsh reality of what you did. And get past it you will.

Even if you stole and was caught, you can get past the pain and shame.

On the road to self-forgiveness you must recognize the extent of the damage you have inflicted.

You can't cringe self-protectingly, in denial and expect to feel good again. You can't dodge behind excuses and self-effacing behavior, and expect to be free of the shame and pain.

If you raped, call yourself a rapist; if you touched inappropriately, call yourself a molester. If you stole, call yourself a thief; if you schemed, call yourself a schemer; if you defrauded, call yourself a fraudster; if you habitually lie, call yourself a liar.

Be merciless in silently acknowledging to yourself—between you and God—responsibility for your conduct. Then, acknowledge audibly, your transgression—again, just between you and God.

Weep, sob, let the pain out, but, Beloved, acknowledge, with no quibbling, what you did.

You are precious; you are valuable; you are sweet, but only you can release the ugliness you feel, the ugliness that keeps on distorting your behavior and polluting your communication.

Realize that your behavior is your presentation of yourself. You alone can fix your behavior.

Acknowledge whatever your problem is, and get past it, once and for all.

Say the words of self-confrontation; repeat them, in a safe place, shout them; magnify them audibly and so release this magnification of your shame, and make way for quiet self-acceptance and peace. Beloved, release is a gift. Claim it.

This is the only way to get past that label and be able with an easy conscience to look back there and say, I violated another's trust and raped, but thank God, I am not now a rapist; I took what was not mine to take, so I was a thief, but thank God, I am not now a thief; I schemed and plotted to defraud, but thank God I am not now a schemer or a fraudster.

If you violated a child who looked to you for protection, a wife who expected respect, or any other whose safety you compromised, you have to find some way to make restitution, or life could bring to you consequences you would want to escape.

One of the consequences of going against the inner law written on the hearts of all—the law of mutual respect—is a revolting conscience. And as the saying goes, "Conscience is a hard taskmaster".

Conscience* can feel merciless, at times.

What is happening between you and your conscience? Do you feel remorse for what you did?

You may try subduing your conscience, what is popularly referred to as hardening your heart, but your personality would be twisted and distorted as conscience whips you behind the repression.

Truly, you might run, but you'd never be able to hide from yourself.

Feelings of remorse are meant to be instructive, not destructive—certainly not self-destructive.

*Note: In time you would need to address this taskmaster (conscience) which sometimes takes you to task not because you are in the wrong but because of how you, perhaps unconsciously, programmed it.

1⁸ Respect Boundaries

Know this—your sexual urges are your concern. Your right to have your sexual needs met ends where the other person's right to be safe from your harassment begins.

You, the perpetrator, are wrong to force yourself on another to satisfy your lusting.

Your sexual needs are your business—your concern, your responsibility. They are not the concern or the responsibility of another.

If you feel sexually aroused, that is your business.

Stay in control of your body. Respect the right of others—even animals—to feel safe within their boundaries—to be safe from your harassment in private or in public.

You won't want any other—animal or human—forcing you into submission to have their sexual or other hunger needs met despite your resistance, fright, and distress.

Do not terrorize another. If you are feeling out of control, go to a psychiatric institution and ask them to admit you for treatment.

Life brings you consequences for the wrong you do, and one of the consequences for disrespecting the right of the other to be safe is a haunting sense of shame, an inability to calmly look yourself, or any other, in the eye.

Relate to others as you would want others relating to you, is a safe rule to live by. This is the essence of the Golden Rule, "Do unto others as you would have them do unto you".

When you violate another, the guilt that distresses you, is genuine guilt—true, justifiable guilt. Such guilt should lead you away from repeating any offensive behavior.

If despite guilt over a past transgression you however still feel driven by urges to violate another, go find a therapist or cleric, and get help to manage your mind and behavior responsibly.

But regardless of your feelings, do not cross the line and interfere with another! Make this a top priority rule in your life—never transgress another's personal boundaries to have any perceived need of yours satisfied. Never!

You have no right to the other person's body, not even to an animal's body!

So, despite the feelings in your body, fix your mind on living honorably; stay in control of your behavior, and make yourself behave appropriately. Make living in integrity a personal rule for managing your life.

Do not lead yourself into temptation.

Your mind is yours to control. Be alert to what you expose it to.

What you expose your senses to will influence what you think about. And you are being challenged to think differently.

Fix your focus on anything wholesome.

Your determination to think differently will strengthen your resolve to live in integrity.

"What you desire most of all is inner peace. And peace comes with soul freedom. And freedom comes with truthfulness." . . . The Author

19 Help All Recover

Witnessing your recovery, many of us feel enabled to attend to our own pain and shame. You help us get out from under the weight of our own guilt. Your healing is like the yeast in the dough. As you grow, we who are observing you, feel more expansive.

Part of the recovery process is facing up to your story and the feelings it evokes in you. Remember, don't hide from your story. Don't pretend that you are perfect. None of us is.

None of us qualifies to point a finger of blame or a finger of condemnation at you, so forget about us, and reclaim your dignity by facing up to your story.

The first step in making things right is you facing up to what you did. This is what the exercise in Chapter Eight allows you to do.

It is very human to excuse self, and to be soft on passing judgment on your own behavior, but do not give in to the temptation to be soft on yourself.

This is not about saving face. This exercise is about you being true to yourself so you could be strong in character and be comfortable in your every moment.

Look clear-eyed at yourself.

Make yourself face the harshness of the glare of that 'shameful' thing you did.

Acknowledge what you did—no white-washing.

This is the first step on the path of healing, acknowledging what your behavior—your presentation of yourself—has been like.

Despairingly holding your head and shutting your eyes will just lead you deeper into self-condemnation.

Now is the time for self-redemption. And all you have to work with is your mind. Whatever you direct your mind to do it will do.

Your imagination (your mind) can transport you into joys you haven't imagined possible; it can also hold you in limiting self-talk.

You are about looking at what you did, accepting that what you did reflected where you were then, and knowing that you are now at a better place or, at least, trying to get to a better place.

You have grown. Now, you are wiser in judgment, and clearer in insight.

What you desire most of all is inner peace. And peace comes with soul freedom. And freedom comes with truthfulness.

No price is too high to pay for soul freedom. And the price you will have to pay would be self-discipline—a gift you will give yourself.

Now, take some time to introspect, but first, relax. Relax your body. Relax your mind.

Shame and pain make you tense.

Hold your body erect. Take some deep breaths. Stretch your body till you get in a few big yawns.

Be alert to how your body is feeling—to how your stomach is feeling, to how your head is feeling. Check out the parts of your body that register discomfort or stress.

Spend time with each area of your body. How are these parts of your body feeling?

What about your posture?

What is happening to your shoulders? Are you upright and stiff, bent over with shoulders hunched?

Is your body feeling relaxed?

Observe your body. Practice keeping your spine straight, and your head erect. Let the prank (life force—the air you take in) flow freely through your tissues.

Be aware that your subconscious thoughts are finding expression in your tissues.

How are you holding your facial muscles, your lips, your eyes?

How is your breathing—shallow, or deep?

How is your chest feeling?

Be aware of what is happening with every part of your body.

Be aware of how interconnected every part (of this wonderful milieu of energy called your body) is with the whole.

What is that nagging thought that despite this exercise, still is keeping you tense? Be alert to how thoughts affect feelings and how feelings control behavior.

This body system has been enabling you to be—to be expressed.

Thank every part, and say thanks for the collaboration of each part in keeping you alive. I often say, "Thanks every cell and cellular product of my body. Thanks, every biochemical pathway, and thanks, energy system of my body. Thanks to every atom and every particle in my body; thanks for maintaining this body in dynamic equilibrium, enabling me to do the work I am here to do."

Go ahead, say thanks to your body. Your word is power. Your body hears.

Now, consciously, relax.

Relax every part of your body.

You think more clearly when your body is relaxed.

If you have offended one, you have offended all of us. You owe it to all of us to make this right, and you can make this right.

Despite what you did, there is room for restitution.

What you did might have been reprehensible, but you are redeemable. Don't make excuses.

If you have made a public example of yourself, then make a public apology. This humbling exercise releases the tension, allowing peace to rush in and fill your soul.

Help another who did wrong to know they can reclaim their dignity by resolving, and following up on your resolve to, from here on, make more responsible choices.

You are not isolated from the rest of us. When you hurt all of us are affected.

When you, embarrassed, indulge in playing hide and seek, with all its dodging antics, all of us see and some of us understand what you are doing.

However, though we may feel compassion for you we cannot stop your game of hiding in shame. Only you can do that.

We long for you to stop playing the games because we feel your discomfort. Just one thing we desire for you—that you live honorably, with self-respect, self-appreciation, and inner comfort.

We who live consciously are not about digging through your past to discover or uncover your imperfections. We are here in celebration of your determination to walk straight from here on. Feel free to come to us. We are not here to condemn you but to support you.

When you accept full responsibility for your conduct, and for what happened to you, the rest of us can breathe easier. Turning your life around can compensate for whatever had you buckled down in shame —can completely compensate!

Face your past. Accept your past as part of your story. Learn from it, and grow.

20 Allow Self To Heal

Healing is yours if you desire it. Pain and shame have no power of their own.

Thinking and behaving differently is the key to living differently. Change of behavior means that you now allow yourself to see other perspectives, and to try out different responses. You become alert to how casually and matter-of-factly you allowed your thinking to direct your behavior along a path that left you feeling guilty and ashamed.

Becoming aware of what in you needs to be changed is of course, a prerequisite to self-healing.

You cannot change without being aware of what it is you must change, and how to locate that thing that must be changed.

Within you is omnipotence. And in omnipotence is truth—truth and power. You are the power. You are not your story. You are the power to create stories to teach yourself lessons you need to learn.

Graduate from the classroom of those stories that taught you painful but necessary lessons.

Beautiful experiences await you but the beauty would be perceived only through your awakened awareness.

Moment to moment, live in conscious awareness of what you are thinking and what you are feeling. Be consciously aware of the source of your power and wisdom. Be alert to how a change in your thinking is being manifested in your living.

Cultivate an attitude of reverence for your mind. What you expose it to will determine the thoughts that would create your moment to moment living. No idle day-dreaming now. No idle mind wandering. Feel your power as you stay alert to what is happening in your mind.

Examine your thoughts and the feelings they generate. Watch how thoughts and feelings can dictate how you behave.

Observe how all this ties in to the values and standards you profess to live by. Stay in conscious awareness of your feelings. Identify immediately the source of any perception of unhappiness, or soul discomfort.

Stay with your thoughts and find the source of any discomfort, even that little niggling uneasiness you feel. Stay with your thoughts till you identify the self-talk that keeps you in distress; then change your self-talk.

You are intrinsically okay but as human you have work to do. You have to take responsibility for experiencing happiness.

If you are reading this material I am taking it for granted that you want a happy life, one free of guilt and shame.

To live free of guilt and shame you must be able to identify how these emotions manifest in your behavior. For example, how does shame distort your behavior? How does guilt affect your interactions?

Do you go into a silent emotional nose dive, beating up on yourself, when you feel publicly or privately condemned, minimized, or demeaned, or when you are fuming over old hurts?

And why would you feel condemned, minimized, or even demeaned? Where do these feelings come from—not from within your own mind—in the constant chatter between you and yourself?

Self-observation, close self-observation, leads to self-understanding.

Nothing bothers you if you are not condemning yourself.

What distresses, or upsets you is not what happened back there. It is definitely not what others have been saying, or thinking about you, or doing to you.

What really has been affecting your life is what you have been saying to yourself about yourself. Let me repeat this—what has been holding you back or pushing you forward is what you have been saying to yourself about yourself.

If your life feels like it has been on hold for just too long, change your self-talk. Shift perspective. Put an end to negativism and self-condemnation. Pay attention to your words.

As awkward as it might feel, change the words—the expressions —that are so easily uttered by you. Word is power. Words have power. They affect your reality.

Listen to yourself. Listen to every word you utter. Note your feelings associated with these expressions. Pay attention to your tone —how you sound.

The deeper you is hearing yourself, and your self is responding through the quality of your life to the unconscious messages you have been unconsciously expressing through your words—whether serious or flippant.

What you have been saying to yourself has you where you are, accounts for how you feel, and for the quality of communication others have been experiencing with you. Move yourself to a brighter reality by consciously expressing encouraging messages. Think optimism. Talk optimism.

Nurture within yourself positive vibrations. Look for the positive —the bright side—in every situation. Talk about goodness. Celebrate goodness in your life.

Pursue the quality of life you want.

Use your mind to create the life you want. This is not idle day dreaming. This is a conscious picturing of what you want for yourself. See it. Visualize it. Dwell on it, and you will materialize it. Your life is in your hands, and your hands are figuratively sustained by God's hands. God is the spirit in you—source of your power to create what you want to materialize.

In every experience is a lesson for you. If you have felt humiliated, know that in humiliation—public or private—can be found the seed of true strength.

To rise from feelings of shame you have to summon your inherent strength. So instead of seeing yourself belittled, see yourself forced to summon your inherent strength.

Instead of feeling demeaned see yourself challenged to accept your intrinsic worth, your beauty, your resilience, regardless of what others say, and regardless of the situation.

Instead of feeling condemned, listen to what was said. If your performance was condemned as not good enough, accept the challenge to do better.

Confront the abysmal feelings of personal unworthiness that send you crashing into self-condemnation when things do not go your way or when others disagree with you.

See no enemies. That person you call enemy is just another soul, like yourself, wanting to be respected, understood, and accepted. Understand that this person is not your problem. Be impervious to the attempt of any to hurt. You cannot feel attacked when you know your true worth. Instead you will see the person who seems to be attacking as another hurting soul who has not yet come to terms with his or her innate strength and beauty.

Any distress you feel is rooted in the way you think—nowhere else.

Your job is laid out for you. You have to work with your thinking. You have to clear your mind of disabling core beliefs.

Set your goal. Prayerfully, persistently, pursue it, and you would achieve it. By then feelings of shame and guilt would have been replaced by acceptance of your inherent ability to rise above all obstacles, including that troubling, haunting sense of self-doubt.

Talk strength to yourself. Your subconscious will believe whatever you habitually tell yourself. Work in your favor—speak strength to yourself.

You are sensible—sensible enough to know your worth, to know that you are too important to spend your life focusing on the ugly when nature is dazzling with beauty.

Let understanding and self-acceptance clear away the hurt and reveal the truth about who you are. You are a vessel of divinity. You carry self-healing powers within you. Change your self-appraisal, and experience healing.

Allow yourself to heal.

2 1 Spirit Enables

Whether or not you acknowledge it, what you need is inner peace. This is what releasing the shame and the pain is about—about living in peace.

In the absence of guilt is peace.

To nurture peace within, consciously live a life of devotion. Wake up with God in your thoughts. Go to bed with God in your mind.

Spend your every moment, regardless of what you are involved in, giving praise and thanks to God.

Fall in love with God, and experience the quiet thrill of counting your blessings and living in a state of continuous thanksgiving.

Live in the heightened awareness that you—your mind and body —are where God is expressed—that mind, body, and soul, you are one with the Eternal.

Consider the implication of this truth.

As you live with the Supreme—God—as your all absorbing focus, at every turn, your life would be guided.

You would discover all things working together for your good— that your love of, and devotion to, God is your guarantee of a secure and harmonious life.

Let every word in your heart and every meditation arising from your soul be harmonious with the vibrations of God within.

When you live this way, wherever you go, God will manifest through you.

Make yourself thoughtful of others, thankful to God, self-respecting and humble in whatever you do, and responsible in your interaction with the environment.

Know that nothing happens just by chance, that every incident has a purpose.

Pursue this thought and you'd realize that everything is interconnected and purposeful, and that there is really no good or bad outcome, just strings of interactions with lessons for all.

Stay in communication with God, passionately in flow with God, then stand back and observe how your thinking (and therefore your life) becomes transformed—how instead of seeing "problems", or "trouble", you see just you seeking to follow where God is leading and life bringing to you guidance through lessons learned in each experience.

Complete surrender is what is expected of you.

Surrender your will to God, and Spirit within will replace the worry in your mind with thanksgiving, praise, and peace.

Let the *Prayer of Serenity* be yours: "God, grant me the Serenity to accept the things I cannot change, Courage to change the things I can, and Wisdom to know the difference."

End

ABOUT THE AUTHOR

Eugenia A. Franklin-Springer

A former university lecturer in Biology (in the Caribbean and in the US), the author became a radio and newspaper family life counselor, and an Internet counselor in abusive relationships. Birthed in Trinidad, the author credits the US as the place of her spiritual rebirth. As a child, she was schooled at Tacarigua EC, Tunapuna Government, and Caribbean Union College (CUC) Elementary in Maracas, St. Joseph. She attended CUC High School, spent her first two years of college at Oakwood College in Huntsville, Alabama, and earned a BSc, MSc, and Ph.D. in Zoology, from Howard University, Washington, D.C. USA.

Her self-assigned life mission has been to know self and know God.

BOOKS BY THIS AUTHOR

The Spiritual Journey/Gethsemane And The Wilderness

Author describes being taken through the ego-scrubbing process of personal transformation, directed by the Inner Guide.

Girl And Her Therapist/Release The Shame

Using psychodrama to address the guilt and shame under which too many victims of sexual abuse cower for too long, the author guides victims and remorseful former abusers, to a new reality of personal freedom

Communication For Survival/It Didn't Have To End So

Author relates two versions of nine stories of typical everyday interactions. In the first version, because of the quality of communication each story has an unfortunate, and in some cases, even a tragic ending. In the second version, by changing the quality of the interpersonal communication, the author shows how each story could have ended differently.

Tantie Pearlie;S Funeral

The cultural norms of village life is beautifully captured in this story of a village community caring for a beloved member through her illness, crowding the little bedroom, tearfully keeping her company through to her last breath, the crossing of a baby over her body as she takes her last breath, the washing, and dressing of her body, and all the rituals and customs followed as family prepares for the procession, church service, and the warm togetherness of the cemetery scene. Tantie Pearlie's Funeral is a semi-fictional story of family, and community bonding as together they lovingly bid farewell to one who had been among them all their life.

Family Relationships/Dear Dr. Springer

Family Life Consultant responds to letters seeking answers to relationship, and personal problems.

Abe & Lucinda/The Curse

Cursed by a sorceress who disrupted his plans to marry his teenage love, Abe mysteriously disappeared. Refusing to give up on searching for the love of her life, Lucinda, twenty tears later, tracks the elderly sorceress to a remote bushy village. She would see Abe, but would he recognize her.

Korruptors/Wrong&Strong

On a tropical island where "money talks", Julia Gordio, a cartel madam is relying on winning a government contract to establish a kidney dialysis center on the island. The contract would give the cover she needs to ditch the insecure arrangement of contracting homeless children divers to collect parcels dropped on the ocean floor. She wins the contract but through chicanery, loses it to an unqualified bidder. Her legal challenge looks promising but just to be sure, she has the winner of the contract kidnapped. The entire country is traumatized by the kidnapping and random bombings that follow as Julia leaves no witnesses. Unknown to her, eyes she thought she had closed forever, are keeping the authorities apprised of her every move.

Words Of A Caribbean Woman (Poetry Of The Author)

The soul of this Caribbean woman captures in poetry, the longings, dreams, and aspirations of of her people . . . searching, searching . . . Who am I? Who are my people? Her search for meaning, and mission, makes of her your sister.

Girl, It's All About You

A guidance book for adolescent girls. Out of print.

Made in the USA
Columbia, SC
09 January 2023

75111783R00065